WITHOUT LIMITS, WHAT CAN KIDS CREATE?

ADVENTURES — IN — ENGINEERING FOR KIDS

35 CHALLENGES TO DESIGN THE FUTURE AS YOU JOURNEY TO CITY X

ROCKPORT

BRETT SCHILKE

Brimming with creative inspiration, how-to projects, and useful information to enrich your everyday life, Quarto Knows is a favorite destination for those pursuing their interests and passions. Visit our site and dig deeper with our books into your area of interest: Quarto Creates, Quarto Cooks, Quarto Homes, Quarto Lives, Quarto Drives, Quarto Explores, Quarto Gifts, or Quarto Kids.

First published in 2020 by Rockport Publishers, an imprint of The Quarto Group, 100 Cummings Center, Suite 265-D, Beverly, MA 01915, USA.
T (978) 282-9590 F (978) 283-2742 QuartoKnows.com

Rockport Publishers titles are also available at discount for retail, wholesale, promotional, and bulk purchase. For details, contact the Special Sales Manager by email at specialsales@quarto.com or by mail at The Quarto Group, Attn: Special Sales Manager, 100 Cummings Center, Suite 265-D, Beverly, MA 01915, USA.

10 9 8 7 6 5 4 3 2

ISBN: 978-1-63159-839-5

Digital edition published in 2020
eISBN: 978-1-63159-840-1

Library of Congress Control Number: 2020930656

Design and Illustration: Headcase Design
Photography: Page 26, Matthew Straub; page 58, Imperial War Museum; page 76, Made In Space, Inc.; pages 92 and 93, City X Project; page 139, Benjamin Quinto; pages 42, 43, 59 (top), 74, 75, 77, 108, 110, and 127 Shutterstock.

"Oops, I dropped the lemon tart" photo by City Foodsters, page 59, is licensed under CC BY 2.0.

Journey to City X™ and Irresistible Futures™ are trademarks of Brett Schilke.

This work is inspired by the story of the City X Project, an Open Education Resource created by Libby Falck, Brett Schilke, and Matthew Straub

Printed in China

TO ANYONE ANYWHERE
WHO HAS EVER BEEN
TOLD WHAT THEIR
FUTURE WILL BE:

DON'T BELIEVE IT.
PROCEED AS IF
SUCCESS IS
INEVITABLE.

CONTENTS

YOUR JOURNEY TO CITY X STARTS HERE...

TRANSMISSION FROM THE MAYOR OF CITY X — 9

ENGINEER BRIEFING — 10

The Irresistible Futures Agency — 10

The Design Process — 12

Seven Social Challenges — 14

Prepare Yourself to Be a Designer of the Future — 16

CHALLENGES

1 DESIGN THE FUTURE OF TRANSPORTATION — 18

Understand the Challenge

Transportation Basics — 19

Explore: Immerse Yourself in the Challenge — 20

User Research: Survey — 22

Synthesize: Create a "What-if" Question — 24

Design a Solution

Case Study: The Importance of Perspective — 26

Imagine: The Blank Page — 28

Create: Improve and Repeat — 30

Share: The Three-Act Story — 32

2 DESIGN THE FUTURE OF ENVIRONMENT — 34

Understand the Challenge

Environment Basics — 35

Explore: My Little Corner of the World — 36

User Research: Vote — 38

Synthesize: The Why Game — 40

Design a Solution

Case Study: Biomimicry — 42

Imagine: The Creative Walk — 44

Create: Build a Prototype — 46

Share: Your Citizen's Irresistible Future — 48

3 DESIGN THE FUTURE OF COMMUNICATION — 50

Understand the Challenge

Communication Basics — 51

Explore: The "What's in My Head?" Game — 52

User Research: Letter Writing — 54

Synthesize: Draw a Problem Map — 56

Design a Solution

Case Study: Innovation by Accident — 58

Imagine: Scrambled Imagination — 60

Create: Blueprint Your Idea — 62

Share: Storyboard — 64

4 DESIGN THE FUTURE OF FOOD — 66

Understand the Challenge

Food Basics — 67

Explore: Make an Empathy Web — 68

User Research: Word On the Street — 70

Synthesize: The Four P's — 72

Design a Solution

Case Study: Building Our New Home World — 74

Imagine: Interconnected Challenges — 78

Create: Clay Modeling — 80

Share: TV Commercial — 82

5   DESIGN THE FUTURE OF HEALTH   84

Understand the Challenge

Health Basics   85

Explore: Your Own Life   86

User Research: Point of Service   88

Synthesize: Think like a Doctor   90

Design a Solution

Case Study: The World's Youngest Space Engineer   92

Imagine: Designing with Constraints   94

Create: Feedback from Everyone   96

Share: A Poetic Solution   98

6   DESIGN THE FUTURE OF ENERGY   100

Understand the Challenge

Energy Basics   101

Explore: Live a Day   102

User Research: Data Analysis   104

Synthesize: First Principles   106

Design a Solution

Case Study: Horse Poop 9 Feet High   108

Imagine: "This is not a . . ."   112

Create: Focus Group   114

Share: Musically Speaking   116

7   DESIGN THE FUTURE OF SAFETY   118

Understand the Challenge

Safety Basics   119

Explore: Safety First   120

User Research: Town Hall   122

Synthesize: Systems Thinking   124

Design a Solution

Case Study: Innovation vs Invention   126

Imagine: Outside the Box   128

Create: Engineer's Choice   130

Share: Your Moment of Fame   132

CONCLUSION

YOUR IRRESISTIBLE FUTURE...

THANK YOU FROM THE MAYOR OF CITY X   135

What Is Your Irresistible Future?   136

Acknowledgments   138

About the Author   139

Index   140

THE JOURNEY TO CITY X

FIVE YEARS AGO, a band of brave and adventurous humans left our planet on a journey to settle a new planet deep in space. With the population of Earth expanding fast and the growing need to preserve our precious natural resources, humanity embarked on a mission to become an interplanetary species.

Like the explorers in the early days of modern civilization on Earth, these humans could not take with them all of the things they would need on the new planet. Instead, they brought tools—like 3D printers, robotic implements, and advanced computing systems—and the knowledge to build what they'd need when they arrived.

The settlers have what they need to build their new city, but now they need creative ideas to help make their new home the best place for the future of humanity.

FROM: MAYOR OF CITY X

Dear Citizens of Earth,

We have arrived at our new home world and have set about creating our first settlement, City X. The journey to City X was a historic one—a journey across the galaxy, a journey that made humans an interplanetary species.

Now that we are getting more comfortable here in City X, our people are excited to create a future that works for everyone. We have begun building some of the things we need, but we have many challenges to solve. These challenges are a lot like the problems we faced on Earth, but here in City X we have the opportunity for a fresh start, to design our world in the best way possible from the very beginning.

We are turning to you, the citizens of Earth, for help. I have just made a proclamation to create a new agency in City X—the Irresistible Futures Agency—made up of young people from around the planet who will be responsible for designing the future of humanity here in City X.

We have the materials we need to produce new things, and we have technology like 3D printers and powerful computing systems. But we need *you*. We need your visions, your ideas, your creativity, and your solutions to the problems we face.

You'll find everything you need included in this transmission. You will meet citizens from City X who are experiencing seven different problems, and we will provide you with all the tools and knowledge you need to understand our challenges and become unstoppable engineers. I will be with you throughout your journey to lend a hand when you need it.

The future of City X—and the future of humanity—is in your hands.

ENGINEER BRIEFING

FOR: EARTH-BASED ENGINEERS FOR CITY X

▸ **WHO**

The Irresistible Futures Agency is made up of a vast team of young engineers from Earth with a mission to create a future that works for everyone in City X.

▸ **WHAT**

Engineers are problem solvers. Sometimes we think of engineers as people who only design machines or airplanes, but they work in all sorts of jobs: in factories, technology companies, schools, governments, and more. The best way to think about an engineer is as a *designer of solutions*, helping create a future that works for everyone.

As an Irresistible Futures engineer, you will learn about the challenges faced in City X, become a master of design, and bring about a bright future for humanity. This Engineer Briefing will teach you the methods and tools that we use as Irresistible Futures agents.

▸ **HOW**

This book contains all the information and knowledge you need to design the future of City X. Each chapter is dedicated to one of seven challenges being faced by the citizens. Study this engineer briefing to understand the information and tasks you are about to encounter.

WHAT DOES *IRRESISTIBLE* MEAN?

If something is irresistible, it means it's impossible to say no to. It is so good, so exciting, and so positive that almost everyone will like it. So an irresistible future is a future that we can't wait to be a part of.

HOW DO WE DESIGN AN IRRESISTIBLE FUTURE?

IN EACH CHAPTER you will find knowledge and activities to help you understand the challenges faced in City X and design solutions for an irresistible future. You will design seven solutions, one for each challenge.

▸ CHALLENGE BASICS

Read these pages carefully to learn simple background information about each type of challenge being faced in City X. You will learn about three elements of each challenge that the citizens of City X are asking engineers to solve.

▸ USER RESEARCH

User research is what engineers do to understand the people who will be using the things they design. User research takes many forms. In each challenge you will learn a new way to put yourself in the shoes of other people and learn the perspectives of five citizens of City X. You will choose one of these citizens to design a solution for.

▸ CASE STUDIES

A case study is a story you can learn from. Usually a case study is about a person, idea, company, or big question, and tells us an important lesson, a unique way of thinking, a science fact we might not know, or how a new tool can be used. You will find seven case studies in this book, one for each challenge in City X. Read the case studies carefully and try to use what you learn as you design solutions for the future of City X.

▸ DESIGN PROCESS ACTIVITIES

Engineers use a special type of problem solving called the design process. The design process has five steps:

EXPLORE · SYNTHESIZE · IMAGINE · CREATE · SHARE

In each chapter you will find five activities—one for each stage of the design process. The activities will help you **understand the challenge** and **design a solution for the future**.

On the next pages you will learn more about each stage of the design process. With each stage you complete, you will come one step closer to being an official Irresistible Futures agent.

THE DESIGN PROCESS

HOW DOES AN ENGINEER DESIGN SOLUTIONS?

One of the tools engineers use to design solutions is the design process. It is a process that helps us understand challenges and find new and powerful ways to solve them.

There are many different ways to use the design process and many different names for it. This is because it is actually a natural way of problem solving that has evolved along with people and society. As you design solutions to the problems faced in City X, you will learn seven different ways to practice each stage of the design process:

EXPLORE   SYNTHESIZE   IMAGINE   CREATE   SHARE

THINKING TO SOLVE PROBLEMS

When we design solutions, we want to consider a lot of ideas but also be very specific about the problem we are solving. To help us do this, we think in different ways.

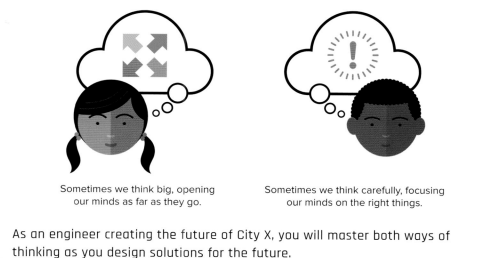

Sometimes we think big, opening our minds as far as they go.

Sometimes we think carefully, focusing our minds on the right things.

As an engineer creating the future of City X, you will master both ways of thinking as you design solutions for the future.

IRRESISTIBLE FUTURES // OUR DESIGN PROCESS

EXPLORE

The **explore** stage is about learning as much as you can about a problem from different points of view. You will learn about the basics of each challenge, study user research, and complete activities that help you know what it's like to be in someone else's shoes.

Collect all of the facts and perspectives

SYNTHESIZE

The **synthesize** stage is about information: organizing it, making sense of it, and deciding what to do with it. You will choose a citizen of City X to design a solution for and set a goal that guides you as an engineer.

Organize knowledge and define a goal to work toward

IMAGINE

The **imagine** stage is when we start to design solutions, and it is all about creativity! Follow four rules to imagine solutions to problems:

1. Come up with as many ideas as possible.
2. Build on the ideas of others!
3. Wild ideas are great.
4. No robots or apps. That's too easy!

Come up with creative ideas

CREATE

The **create** stage is a process of building models (called prototypes) and testing them to get feedback from other people. In the create phase you will complete activities that make your ideas come to life so you can make them even better.

Choose your favorite idea and begin to build and test it to make it better

SHARE

The **share** stage is about communicating your ideas to the world. In the share stage, you will complete activities that help you tell the story of your challenge, your solution, and the irresistible future it will create.

Share your story with as many people as possible

ENGINEER BRIEFING

As an Irresistible Futures engineer, you will design solutions to challenges faced by the citizens of City X, the first human settlement on a new planet. The citizens have identified seven major social problems they are facing as they create their new city. To each agent, we ask one question:

"What if we could solve the biggest challenges in City X and design a future that works for everyone?"

LEARN ABOUT THE SEVEN SOCIAL CHALLENGES

TRANSPORTATION
How we get around and move things

ENVIRONMENT
Everything that surrounds us, from the air to the trees to the buildings

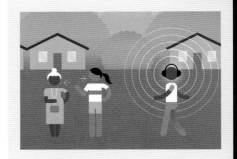

COMMUNICATION
How we stay connected to other people

FOOD
How we keep ourselves strong

HEALTH
How we keep ourselves from getting sick

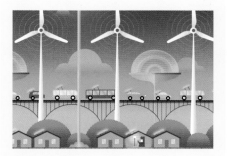

ENERGY
How we make ourselves productive and comfortable

SAFETY
How we protect ourselves, our friends, and our world

TEST YOUR KNOWLEDGE

SOCIAL PROBLEMS VS. PERSONAL PROBLEMS

A social problem is a problem that affects a lot of people, such as a whole community or even a whole planet. These are important problems to solve to make life better for everyone.

A personal problem is a problem that is experienced by just one person. These problems might seem important to us if we are experiencing them, but usually solving them will only help one person.

We want to use our creativity to solve social problems. Which of these problems are social problems?

A.	B.	C.	D.

Erin is hungry.	There is no food in our stores.	The power has been out for two weeks.	Shailesh's phone is dead.

Answers: B, C

ENGINEER PREPARATION

PREPARE YOUR TOOLS

There are two things that every engineer needs to do his or her job.

DESIGN NOTEBOOK
& PEN OR PENCIL

It is also good to have a special design kit that helps you make ideas come to life. Ask an adult you trust to help you find as many of these things as you can and remember where they are as you design solutions. If you can't find something, that's okay. You will use what you have!

> You are almost ready to begin designing solutions for the future of City X. Do you remember what you have learned so far? Answer these questions to continue:
>
> 1. What is your mission from the citizens of City X?
>
> 2. What are the five steps of the Irresistible Futures Design Process?

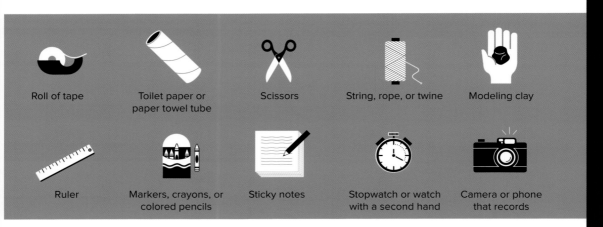

| Roll of tape | Toilet paper or paper towel tube | Scissors | String, rope, or twine | Modeling clay |
| Ruler | Markers, crayons, or colored pencils | Sticky notes | Stopwatch or watch with a second hand | Camera or phone that records |

You'll find these pictures on each Design Process Activity, so you will always know which tools you need to complete a task.

You will also see these pictures, which are important instructions for some activities:

 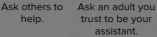

| Use your designer brain! | Ask others to help. | Ask an adult you trust to be your assistant. | Ask permission from an adult you trust. | Safety | The amount of time you'll need |

CREATE YOUR DESIGN NOTEBOOK

The design notebook is very important. It is where you will keep all of your notes, ideas, and solutions for problems in City X. Any notebook will work, as long as it has at least fifty pages.

1 MAKE IT YOUR OWN

You can decorate your design notebook however you want. It only needs to say two things: your name and "Design Notebook."

2 ORGANIZE YOUR THOUGHTS

Keep your notebook organized. You will have seven challenges and five steps to complete in each one. Label your pages and make sure you can go back to find things later. Each activity will give instructions on how to prepare your notebook.

3 KEEP IT SAFE

Your ideas are important for the future of City X. Make sure you keep your notebook handy to write down any new thoughts that come into your mind, and keep your notebook somewhere safe.

READY?

Your first challenge has been prepared. Turn the page to begin your journey as an engineer of an irresistible future for City X.

DESIGN THE FUTURE OF TRANSPORTATION

TRANSPORTATION GETS US from one place to another, like when we ride our bike down the street, take a car to visit relatives, or get on a train or a plane to go to a new city. Transportation comes with a lot of challenges, and leaving Earth and building a city on a new planet adds even more! Not only do the citizens of City X need to think of how to build transportation for the new city, but they also need to think about space transportation and new types of energy that might be available on their new home world.

The citizens of City X have asked you, the Irresistible Futures agent, to think about three main things when designing the future of transportation:

ELEMENT 1: SPEED

Speed is important when we travel across long distances, but it can be hard if the land, sea, or even air is difficult to cross. **How could we build new kinds of transportation that can go fast and stay clear of the obstacles we find along the way?**

ELEMENT 2: EFFICIENCY

The citizens of City X think that transportation can be a lot more effective than it is on Earth. **How could we make transportation that uses less energy, doesn't pollute the environment, and can get the people who use it to the places they need to go as simply as possible?**

ELEMENT 3: ACCESSIBILITY

There is a lot of open space in City X, so people sometimes live far away. The citizens are all different ages and have different abilities too. **How could we make a transportation system that everyone can use, no matter their age, location, health, or wealth?**

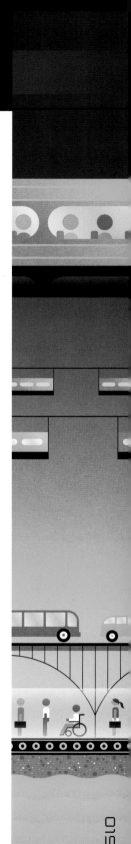

EXPLORE — ACTIVITY

IMMERSE YOURSELF IN THE CHALLENGE

NOW THAT YOU have studied the basics of the transportation challenge, let's get to know it a bit better. One way to **explore** as a designer of solutions is to immerse yourself in the challenge.

Your own community uses transportation in many ways. But how much do you know about the kind of transportation that is used? Ask a trusted adult to spend some time with you exploring your own neighborhood or city and make careful notes about the kinds of transportation you see being used.

PREPARATION

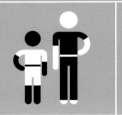

30 MINUTES

▶ WHAT YOU WILL NEED

▶ PREPARE YOUR NOTEBOOK

1 In this activity, we will document information using a simple method of data collection. First, think of as many kinds of transportation as you can. Use the picture here to help you get started.

2 Next, using your design notebook, write these down. Ask an adult you trust for help if you need it. Leave some space between each one to record your observations.

car   train
bus
bicycle
unicycle
skateboard
feet

EXPLORE YOUR NEIGHBORHOOD

Ask an adult you trust to take a walk or a drive in your neighborhood and, each time you see one of these types of transportation, make a mark in your notebook.

TAKE NOTES

At the end of your journey, ask yourself some questions and make notes in your notebook.

▶ **Which type of transportation is the most common where you live?**

▶ **Think about each kind of transportation, one at a time. Is it fast? Is it efficient? Is it accessible? Look back at the first page of this section to refresh your memory about what these words mean.**

▶ **How did you get around during this activity? What were some of the problems that you found with your own kind of transportation?**

REFLECT

In your notebook, write down three things you learned about transportation that you didn't know before.

USER RESEARCH: SURVEY

WHEN YOU THINK about a challenge like transportation, it is important to think about the problem not just from your own perspective but from the perspective of others.

An important part of design is **user research**. This is how you build understanding and empathy for the people who are experiencing a problem. You learn what it is like to be in their shoes, and then you can know better how to make a solution. We surveyed the citizens of City X to learn more about their perspectives on the challenge of transportation. Some of the results from the survey are here, and five of the citizens shared their points of view for the engineering team on Earth.

RESULTS

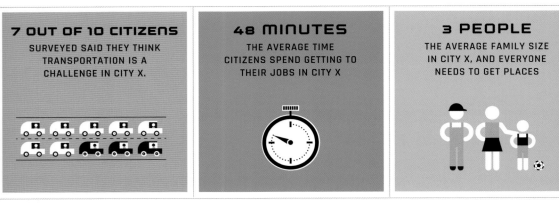

7 OUT OF 10 CITIZENS
SURVEYED SAID THEY THINK TRANSPORTATION IS A CHALLENGE IN CITY X.

48 MINUTES
THE AVERAGE TIME CITIZENS SPEND GETTING TO THEIR JOBS IN CITY X

3 PEOPLE
THE AVERAGE FAMILY SIZE IN CITY X, AND EVERYONE NEEDS TO GET PLACES

SURVEY

One form of user research is the **survey**. A survey is a set of questions that are asked to a group of people in order to understand their perspectives or opinions on a topic. Surveys are often only given to what is called a "representative sample," that is, a small group in a population that is made up of all the same kinds of people as the whole population. In City X there are people from every major culture on Earth, so the survey includes people from all different backgrounds.

Surveys can be made on the internet (making them very easy to distribute), or they can be done in person. You ask everyone the same questions to make sure your results are accurate.

Surveys are good for

1. Asking questions to a lot of people quickly

2. Understanding what a big group of people thinks, by asking questions to a diverse but small group of people

3. Getting data about a problem and learning the opinions that people have

USER RESEARCH: CITIZEN PERSPECTIVES

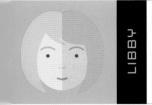

LIBBY

"To get to work every day,
I have to walk 20 minutes to the bus stop."

"My family all needs to go to different places
at different times. How can we all get
where we need to be on our own?"

QUYNH

THET

"There is too much traffic in City X."

"Earth is so far away, and it would be nice to see
my family more often."

CSONGOR

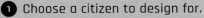

MATTHEW

"My kids need to go places without me, but I don't
think our transportation is easy and safe enough."

WHICH CITIZEN OF CITY X WILL YOU DESIGN FOR?

As an Irresistible Futures agent, you will design a solution for one of these City X citizens. Who will it be?

1 Choose a citizen to design for.

2 How do you think your citizen is feeling? Choose from some of the words to the right or come up with your own.

FRUSTRATED	TIRED
SAD	BORED
BUSY	EXCITED
CONFUSED	HAPPY

SYNTHESIZE ACTIVITY

CREATE A "WHAT-IF" QUESTION

THE **SYNTHESIZE** STAGE is about organizing information, making sense of it, and deciding what to do with it next. In this activity we will practice a skill you will use after every synthesize stage: writing a "what-if" question.

A "WHAT-IF" QUESTION IS A BOLD GOAL FOR THE FUTURE THAT TURNS A *PROBLEM* INTO A *POSSIBILITY*.

A PROBLEM
is a negative story about what today is like.

A POSSIBILITY
is a positive story about what the future can be like.

When we think about **problems**, we can get stuck thinking about how big the problems are or arguing about what is causing them.

But when we think about **possibilities**, we get excited thinking of all the ways we could make that future come true.

We change a problem to a possibility by asking, "What if the world was different?"

Before we set off to solve the problem of your City X citizen, we need to turn that problem into a possibility.

PREPARATION

20 MINUTES

▶ WHAT YOU WILL NEED

▶ PREPARE YOURSELF

1 Think carefully about your citizen and his or her problem.

2 Get ready to flip your thinking toward possibility.

THINK ABOUT YOUR CITIZEN'S FUTURE

A "what-if" question is not about the problem your citizen is facing, and it is not about the solution you are going to create. It is about **describing the future world where your citizen no longer has his or her problem.**

ASK YOURSELF, "HOW IS THAT WORLD DIFFERENT?"

What is that future like? What would be different about life in that future if your citizen no longer had his or her problem?

WRITE A "WHAT-IF" QUESTION

Next, try writing a sentence about that future, asking, "What if . . . ."

Here are some examples of some "what-if" questions other Irresistible Futures engineers have written:

> **"What if anyone could get an education, no matter where they live?"**
>
> **"What if you didn't need to go to the hospital to get healed?"**
>
> **"What if we could grow up without fear?"**

A good "what-if" question should:

1. **Set a goal and a vision for the future**
2. **Spark creative ideas**

EXAMPLE

To learn how to do this, let's think about the problem of **pollution**.

> **PROBLEM**
> "Our world is dirty because of pollution."

When we talk about pollution, it can make us sad to think about how dirty our environment is today. We might argue about what is causing pollution and what the right way to fix it is.

How do we turn that **problem** into **possibility**? If we follow these steps, we can ask, "What if the world was different?" and make a bold statement about what the future could be like.

> **POSSIBILITY**
> "What if we could have clean air and water for our children?"

WRITE YOUR "WHAT-IF..." QUESTION

Turn your citizen's problem into a possibility. With all the new knowledge you have gained, write your own "what-if" question to share the possibility you see for the future of transportation in City X.

THE IMPORTANCE OF PERSPECTIVE

EACH CHALLENGE INCLUDES user research because it is important to understand every challenge from different perspectives. When you put yourself in someone else's shoes, you see challenges in new ways, you understand challenges better, and you can think of better solutions that will work for more people. It's not just the citizens' perspectives that are important, though. You have a unique experience and point of view too.

▸ THET'S PERSPECTIVE

In the user research for this challenge, you met Thet. He shares his perspective that there is too much traffic in City X. Maybe you live in a big city and you understand Thet's perspective very well.

But what if you don't? What if you're not sure what that is like?

▸ EEK, ALASKA

Thet's challenge about traffic was sent to a young agent who lives in the small village of Eek, Alaska. One of the early Irresistible Futures scouting teams visited Eek in order to find agents with unique perspectives to join the engineering team for City X.

When the designer in Eek read Thet's perspective, she made a strange face and asked, "What is traffic?"

"What is traffic?"

CASE STUDY /// WELCOME TO EEK, ALASKA

a story from a City X designer

Eek is home to about 300 people who live on the Alaskan tundra and lead a sustainable, independent life. The village has no roads and no cars, but it is connected to the world with a good school, mobile phones, fast internet, a busy river, and small airplanes that fly to the larger towns. But **traffic** was something Eek had never seen. The idea of traffic wasn't part of life in Eek like it is in other parts of the world.

Thet continued to explain his challenge to the young designer. He talked to her about roads full of cars, about how hard it is to get from one place to another quickly, and compared it to other things that she might have experienced. The first suggestion didn't work, but the second one was perfect.

THINK ABOUT IT

How would you explain to someone a problem they have never experienced?

"What would you do if you had to get from one side of the room to the other but lots of people were in the way?"

"I would say excuse me."

"What if you needed to get somewhere on the river but there were too many boats in the way?"

"Oh! I understand!"

THE SOLUTION

The answer from Eek was surprising to Thet. He thought that it was important to always be on time and rush from one place to another, and that sitting and doing nothing was a bad thing. The perspective from Eek, where life is slower and more comfortable, made him understand his own perspective better.

*** TO THET: "What if we could enjoy our time in traffic?" ***

The engineer in Eek wrote a very unique "what-if" question for Thet. From this designer's perspective, an Irresistible Future was actually about using time, and she created a solution that would help Thet use time in traffic to relax and have fun.

TAKEAWAY

The more perspectives we can gather about a problem, the more we understand the challenge and the more we understand ourselves.

IMAGINE — ACTIVITY

THE BLANK PAGE

THE IMAGINE STAGE is a really fun part. It is all about coming up with ideas!

What would you design to make your "what-if" question come true?

One of the hardest parts of creating solutions and making new things is *starting*. We all know how to use our imaginations, but when we know we are working to fix something important, we start doubting ourselves.

Even for adults, staring at a blank page that we need to fill is scary. In this activity you are going to tackle that idea the only way you can: by taking a deep breath and making the first mark.

Is it the *right way*? What if I mess up? Will people like it? Is this the best I can do? Where should I start?

PREPARATION

20 MINUTES

▶ WHAT YOU WILL NEED

▶ PREPARE YOURSELF

Sometimes it helps to have a little talk with ourselves before we start something hard. So before you start to imagine the future of transportation in City X, do this:

1 Write across the top of your blank page: I CAN IMAGINE . . .

2 Say as loud as you can, say it to the world, "I AM AN ENGINEER! I AM A DESIGNER OF THE FUTURE!"

I CAN IMAGINE...

I am an engineer! I am a designer of the future!

REMIND YOURSELF OF YOUR GOAL

Look back at your "what-if" statement and think hard about it for one minute. How would you make that future come true?

Let your mind dream and wander and think. **Don't hold back!**

MAKE YOUR FIRST MARK

Put your pencil or marker to the center of the paper and just scribble something. Anything. A word. A shape. A big line. Whatever comes through you.

WHEN YOU IMAGINE:

1. COME UP WITH AS MANY IDEAS AS POSSIBLE.
2. BUILD ON THE IDEAS OF OTHERS!
3. WILD IDEAS ARE GREAT.
4. NO ROBOTS OR APPS. THAT'S TOO EASY!

LET YOUR IDEAS FLOW

Hooray! The page isn't blank anymore, so now we don't have to worry. Now try to fill the page with as many ideas as you can. You can write or draw—whatever you prefer. Set a timer for 5 minutes and try to fill your entire page with ideas before your time is up!

CHOOSE YOUR FAVORITE IDEA

Remember, you can always improve your ideas later, so pick the one you are most excited about now!

Circle your favorite idea in your notebook, and now let's get ready to bring it to life.

CREATE  ACTIVITY

IMPROVE AND REPEAT

YOU'VE CHOSEN YOUR best idea. It's time to turn it into reality!

The **create** stage is made up of three parts:

1. Make a model of your idea.
2. Test your idea.
3. Improve and repeat.

An engineer's first idea will never be the final idea. Making something new means you have to make a lot of models and ask a lot of questions, so models are best when they are very simple. Engineers test their ideas many times, asking people each time how they can make their solutions better and stronger. This is a process called **iteration**.

PREPARATION

30 MINUTES

▶ WHAT YOU WILL NEED

▶ MAKE AN IMPROVE-AND-REPEAT PAGE

1 Draw three boxes down the left side of your page.

2 Next to the first and second box, draw a plus sign, a triangle, and a question mark.

3 Next to the third box, leave the area blank.

You'll use this kind of page in every **create** activity, anytime you see "Improve and Repeat."

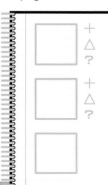

MAKE A MODEL OF YOUR IDEA

Remember that simple models are great, because you use them to help explain your idea and you can change them easily.

A lot of the engineers and designers who work on transportation challenges today design things like cars and buses. When they start to design, they make simple black-and-white marker drawings. There are no colors, no details—just shapes that help someone understand what the solution will be. They can add labels as well to explain how the idea will work.

In your first box in your notebook, draw a simple sketch of your idea.

MAKE YOUR IDEA BETTER

Now it's time to test your idea. Find some friends or an adult you trust and ask them if they would like to help you make your idea better. Tell them three things, using your black-and-white sketch to help:

1. What is the problem you decided to solve?

2. What is your "what-if" question?

3. What is your solution?

Next to the box in your notebook, write down the things you hear from them.

By the plus sign, write things they like.

By the triangle, write things they think should change.

By the question mark, write questions they asked you that you didn't expect.

IMPROVE AND REPEAT

Think about the things people told you about your idea. How can their suggestions and questions make your idea better?

In the second box, draw a new model of your idea that includes some of the feedback from your friends or family.

Repeat the process.

NAME YOUR SOLUTION

In the final box at the bottom of the page, draw the last version of your model. Now it's time to give it a name! What do you call your solution? Write the name next to the last box.

SHARE ——— ACTIVITY

THE THREE-ACT STORY

NOW THAT YOUR idea has been tested and perfected, it is time to share your solution and help people understand how it will solve the transportation problem. The **share** stage is always built on what we call "the three-act story."

This method of sharing your ideas is thousands of years old. It helps people understand where we are coming from, where we are going, and how we will get there. And it's easy!

PREPARATION

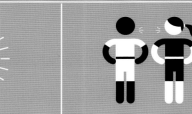

30 MINUTES

▶ WHAT YOU WILL NEED

▶ MAKE A THREE-ACT STORY PAGE

1. Divide your page into three sections.
2. Label the first section "PROBLEM."
3. Label the second section "FUTURE."
4. Label the third section "SOLUTION."

You'll use this kind of page in every **share** activity, anytime you see "three-act story page."

YOUR CITIZEN AND THE PROBLEM

Remind yourself about the original problem. Who are you designing a solution for? What were they feeling and experiencing in City X? Stories are always the best when they are about a **person**, so we always share our ideas from the perspective of the person who will use them.

Make notes in the "PROBLEM" section of your notebook.

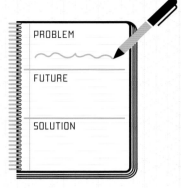

YOUR CITIZEN IN THE FUTURE

Think about your "what-if" statement. What is the irresistible future you are creating for City X by designing this solution? What will the future look like now that your solution exists? How will life be different for your citizen?

Make notes in the "FUTURE" section of your notebook.

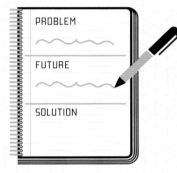

YOUR CITIZEN AND YOUR SOLUTION

Now think about how your citizen will use your solution. What will it look like and feel like to use it? Is it easy to use? What are the features of it?

Make notes in the "SOLUTION" section of your notebook.

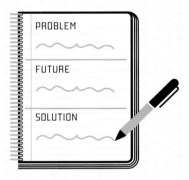

TELL YOUR STORY

Use these notes to share the story of the solution you've created. Be proud of your ideas!

CONGRATULATIONS

You have helped create an irresistible future for **transportation** in City X.

THE
IRRESISTIBLE
FUTURES
AGENCY

2 DESIGN THE FUTURE OF ENVIRONMENT

THE ENVIRONMENT CHALLENGE is about how we take care of everything around us. Sometimes we think of the environment as just water, trees, air, and animals—the natural environment—but it is also about the environment we build, like the buildings and roads in our communities and the different kinds of machines we use to help us live our lives. The citizens of City X have a unique opportunity to plan ahead and start fresh, creating an environment that is healthy for all living things, and to protect their new home world for future generations. How will you help design this future environment that works for everyone?

The citizens of City X have asked you, the Irresistible Futures agent, to think about three main things when designing the future environment:

ELEMENT 1: POLLUTION

Pollution has a big impact on the environment. Many of our machines, processes, and activities on Earth poison our natural environment with chemicals, toxins, and garbage. **How will you help the citizens of City X do all the things they need to and have a future environment that is clean?**

ELEMENT 2: DISASTERS

The citizens of City X want to protect the environment, but it is also something they need to be protected from. Disasters—like bad storms, earthquakes, and fires—are a natural part of all environments. **How will you help the citizens of City X live safely in their future environment?**

ELEMENT 3: BUILT ENVIRONMENT

The built environment, like roads and buildings, is important too. After all, these are the places where people spend a lot of time. **How will you help the citizens of City X build a city that works together with the natural environment to create a healthy and responsible way of life?**

EXPLORE ———— ACTIVITY

MY LITTLE CORNER OF THE WORLD

ONE WAY TO **explore** as a designer of solutions is to observe. When you observe, you watch something, take careful notes, and learn new things. Since we are designing for the future of the environment in City X, in this activity we will spend some time observing the environment near you. Let's get outside!

PREPARATION

10 MINUTES ON THREE DIFFERENT DAYS

▶ WHAT YOU WILL NEED ▶ FIND YOUR CORNER OF THE WORLD

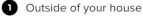

For this activity, go outside with an adult you trust and find a "little corner of the world" that will be yours for the next while. You will be observing this place carefully as a way to learn more about the environment where you live. It is the easiest to pick a place close to home so you can get there quickly and often.

Your corner does not need to be anything special. It could be a quiet area on a walking path, the sidewalk at a street corner, a part of your garden, or anywhere else! There are only a few rules for what your little corner needs to be:

1 Outside of your house

2 Nearby so you can see it often

3 Small enough to see it all at once

If for any reason you cannot go outside, look out a window and find a little corner of the world that can be yours. Make sure you can see it clearly.

1 OBSERVE YOUR CORNER OF THE WORLD

The first time you go to your little corner of the world, observe it carefully. You should know it very well. Here are some things to think about while you are in your space:

1. What life do you see in your little corner of the world? Animals? Plants? Humans?

2. Is it clean?

3. What is the weather like there?

4. What is the environment around it like? Busy or calm?

5. Where is it? In a city? In nature?

2 COME BACK OFTEN TO SEE HOW IT CHANGES

For one week, come back to your little corner of the world often. You can make each visit fast—just a few minutes! But you want to **explore** the environment in your little corner of the world, so you need to see how it changes over time.

3 TAKE NOTES

Each time you come back to your little corner of the world, take notes about what has changed and what has stayed the same. What do you notice about the environment in your corner? Think about the perspectives you learned from citizens in City X. Do you see any of these challenges in your corner?

REFLECT

After a week of visiting your little corner of the world, you probably feel like it is really yours.

In your notebook, write down three things you learned about the environment that you didn't know before.

USER RESEARCH: VOTE

REMEMBER THAT IT is important to think about creating the future of the environment from a lot of different perspectives. Everyone has their own feelings about what needs to be solved.

User research in City X has told us what many citizens think about the environment. They have told us what it is like to experience the challenge from their point of view and what they would like to see solved. To understand the perspectives on the environment in City X, we took a vote about the problems that are most important. Some of the results of the vote are here, and five of the citizens shared their opinions about the future of the environment with our design research team.

RESULTS

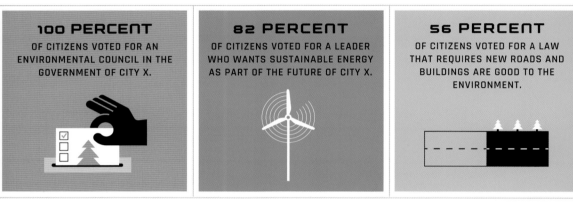

100 PERCENT
OF CITIZENS VOTED FOR AN ENVIRONMENTAL COUNCIL IN THE GOVERNMENT OF CITY X.

82 PERCENT
OF CITIZENS VOTED FOR A LEADER WHO WANTS SUSTAINABLE ENERGY AS PART OF THE FUTURE OF CITY X.

56 PERCENT
OF CITIZENS VOTED FOR A LAW THAT REQUIRES NEW ROADS AND BUILDINGS ARE GOOD TO THE ENVIRONMENT.

VOTE

A common form of user research is a **vote**. Voting is very popular on Earth to help large groups of people make decisions together. In a perfect vote, every person that the decision affects will share their choice. A vote is often used to select leaders or to decide about new laws and rules. Usually in a vote, the majority decision is the winning decision. That means that the choice more people want is the choice that is made, but of course, people often disagree, which means that not everyone will get what they want.

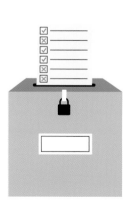

A vote is good for

1. Helping every person have a voice in a decision

2. Making difficult choices that affect a big group of people

3. Deciding between just a couple clear options

USER RESEARCH: CITIZEN PERSPECTIVES

MARIO
"Could our homes and buildings be more friendly to the natural world?"

CASSIDY
"There are big storms in City X, and we are not prepared for them."

ATSA
"I wish we could get around without covering our new world in concrete."

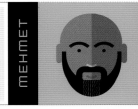

MEHMET
"I want to have clean air and water for my children."

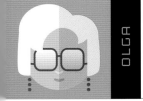

OLGA
"Nature in City X has never been disturbed. We should protect it."

WHICH CITIZEN OF CITY X WILL YOU DESIGN FOR?

As an Irresistible Futures agent, you will design a solution for one of these City X citizens. Who will it be?

1 Choose a citizen to design for.

2 How do you think your citizen is feeling? Choose from some of the words to the right or come up with your own.

HOPEFUL	CONCERNED
ANGRY	RESPONSIBLE
PROTECTIVE	CAUTIOUS
LOVING	SILLY

SYNTHESIZE ACTIVITY

THE WHY GAME

WHEN WE SYNTHESIZE, we think carefully. We try to understand a challenge more deeply by organizing what we know and asking good questions. And one of the most important questions to ask is "why?"

The magic thing about "why?" is that it is the only question in the world that will always have an answer, no matter how many times you ask it. There is a reason for everything.

When you ask "why?" enough times, though, you might find that you have trouble finding the next answer or that the same answer keeps coming up. This is when you know you have found the "root cause." Just like the roots of a tree go deeper and keep branching off into smaller parts, the causes for problems do, too. The root cause is often a good thing to fix! In this activity, we'll practice finding the root cause by playing a game.

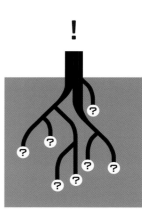

PREPARATION

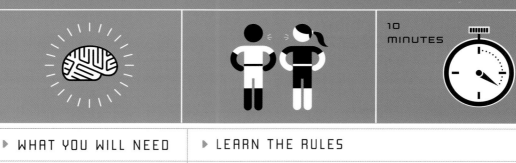

10 MINUTES

▸ WHAT YOU WILL NEED

▸ LEARN THE RULES

The Why Game is very easy to play. All you need is a problem, two people, some brains, and some patience.

1 Find a partner to play with. An adult you trust will be the best.

2 Ask that person to help you better understand the problem your City X citizen is facing.

3 Stop asking questions when you have found your "root cause."

1 ASK YOUR PARTNER ABOUT THE PROBLEM

Share your citizen's problem with your partner. Ask him or her a "why" question, like this:

EXAMPLE

"There is too much traffic in City X."

Do you remember Thet? Let's use him as an example. We'll ask, **"Why do we have a traffic problem?"**

Listen carefully to your partner's answer.

2 ASK "WHY?" AGAIN

Now the rest is simple! Just ask "Why?" again and again until you find that the same answer keeps coming up or there are no more answers to be had. Once you get there, you've found the "root cause."

3 THINK ABOUT THE ROOT CAUSE

How does this game make you think about your citizen's problem differently? Sometimes just by asking "why?" a few times, we find parts of problems that we never noticed before or we realize the problem is being caused by something we didn't think about.

The **synthesize** stage is all about knowing that we are solving the right problem, so these questions are helpful!

WRITE YOUR "WHAT-IF..." QUESTION

Turn your citizen's problem into a possibility. With all the new knowledge you have gained, write your own "what-if" question to share the possibility you see for the future of the environment in City X.

CASE STUDY

BIOMIMICRY

WHEN ENGINEERS DECIDE what a solution looks like and how it will work, they often look at the world around them for inspiration. This means looking at things we make ourselves, but it also means looking at nature.

▶ ARE COMPLICATED SOLUTIONS BETTER?

Sometimes when we try to solve a problem, we think that we need to make our solutions complex. The more pieces and parts, the better! But more often, simple solutions are the best. Simple solutions are easier to explain. Simple solutions focus on fixing one problem well, rather than fixing lots of problems at once.

In this case study, we are going to look at **biomimicry**—how some of nature's simple solutions have inspired real-world engineers to create solutions.

Mimic means to copy. Bio is a short way of saying "biological," which is a way to describe things we find in nature. So *biomimicry* is "copying nature!"

THINK ABOUT IT

Look around you. **How many things can you see right now that were engineered?** That means anything that a person made. Even something as simple as a pencil or a piece of paper was made by an engineer.

How many things can you see right now that were made by nature?

CASE STUDY /// FLIGHT

▶ IT'S A BIRD! IT'S A PLANE!

In the previous chapter, you learned all about the transportation problem. One way we solve this problem on Earth is with airplanes. Today airplanes are common and we don't think much about how or why they work. But did you know that early engineers designing airplanes were inspired by birds?

Many people tried and failed, but eventually we learned the science of how birds fly—and flight for humans became a lot easier. Think about airplanes today. They have a head, two wings, and a tail! Just like nature's simple solution to soar above the Earth.

CASE STUDY ///
VELCRO BRAND FASTENERS

▸ A STICK THAT DOESN'T STOP

Have you ever worn a pair of shoes with a hook-and-loop strap? Or have you adjusted the back of a baseball cap to fit you better? Then you have used a biomimicry design!

In the 1940s, an engineer in Switzerland was taking his dog for a walk and noticed that there were small burrs from a plant that got stuck very securely in his dog's fur. He could get them out by pulling firmly, but they would stick again if they were put back.

The scientist removed the burrs carefully and looked at them under a microscope. He saw tiny hooks on the burrs and was inspired. If he could perfect this design, he could sell it as a system for holding things together securely but also allowing them to be moved.

That innovation, which he named Velcro (a combination of the two French words that mean "velvet" and "hook"), still exists today and is used all around the world to stick things together.

CASE STUDY /// NEEDLES

▸ THE MEDICINAL MOSQUITO

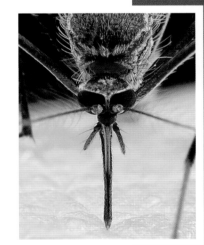

Have you ever seen someone donate blood, or have you gone to the doctor and had them take blood from your body for tests? It can be scary to be poked with a needle, but it's an important way of making sure people stay healthy.

It used to be very difficult to take blood from our bodies, until scientists looked at how nature does it.

Have you ever been bitten by a mosquito? Mosquitos love to drink blood, and they have highly efficient needle-like mouths that pierce the skin and pull blood from animals, including humans. Mosquitos pierce the skin with minimal pain. Sometimes you don't even know you've been bitten until your skin starts itching!

The design of modern medical needles is inspired by mosquitos. These needles reduce pain and draw blood more efficiently. So the next time you hear a mosquito buzzing around your head, tell it "Thank you!" for helping make us all healthier.

TAKEAWAY

When we create solutions, there is beauty in simplicity and strength in nature. Start with basic shapes as the building blocks for creations and be inspired by how nature tackles challenges.

IMAGINE · ACTIVITY

THE CREATIVE WALK

THE CITIZENS OF City X love designs that are inspired by nature. It reminds them of home, and as you learned in the case study, a lot of engineering uses biomimicry as a way of creating new solutions that copy nature's way of solving problems.

For this activity we will do something a little bit different. We will take a walk, much like the inventor of Velcro did when he happened upon his unexpected breakthrough.

PREPARATION

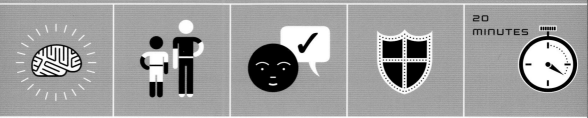

20 MINUTES

▶ WHAT YOU WILL NEED

▶ FLASH LEARNING

Did you know that taking a walk and getting out in nature actually makes us healthier and our brains work better? Sometimes we come up with our best ideas when we are **not** thinking about a problem because our brains work in the background and we make connections when we aren't expecting it.

For the creative walk, it is important to be relaxed and have as much time as you need. Do something that helps you relax for a little while: listen to music, play a game, exercise. Then find a time when you go outside with an adult you trust.

① TAKE A WALK

The first step is so easy! Just take a walk! No matter where you are, movement and energy are great for helping our brains be creative. It doesn't need to be anywhere special; it just needs to be outside. As you are taking your walk, look around you and think about all the ways that nature solves problems. Do you see any of the examples of biomimicry we learned about?

② TAKE NOTES

As you are walking, keep your notebook and writing utensil handy. Make any notes that come to your mind, especially if you suddenly have ideas about the problem you have chosen to solve.

③ COME HOME AND IDEATE

When you get back from your walk, get a blank page ready!

Remind yourself of your citizen's problem and your "what-if" question.

In your notebook, come up with as many ideas as you can to solve your citizen's problem and make your "what-if" question come true.

Remember the rules of ideation:

1. Come up with as many ideas as possible.
2. Build on the ideas of others!
3. Wild ideas are great.
4. No robots or apps—that's too easy!

CHOOSE YOUR FAVORITE IDEA

What new ideas did you come up with that you would not have had before your walk? Select your favorite idea and get ready to create!

CREATE | ACTIVITY

BUILD A PROTOTYPE

YOU'VE SELECTED YOUR best idea. Now it is time to turn it into reality!

You learned in the previous chapter that we start by creating simple models so that we can **iterate**, or make multiple versions as we keep improving our idea. Another way to make models is by making a basic prototype—the first version of an object that you make using things you'll find around your house or your school. So for this activity, we'll build a simple model of our idea using the things we have already.

PREPARATION

			45 MINUTES

▶ WHAT YOU WILL NEED

▶ PREPARE YOURSELF

Before we get started, assemble your full engineer kit. You don't need to have everything listed, and you can also use other things you might find! Ask an adult you trust to help you find things you can build with safely.

1 BUILD YOUR MODEL

Think about what your solution looks like in your mind. Go ahead—close your eyes and imagine it! Now think about the things in your house you could use to make it.

EXAMPLE: Pretend you want to build a rocket and you are going to make a prototype out of things you'll find around the house. What could you use to make it?

2 BUILD YOUR PROTOTYPE

Using materials in your engineer tool kit, build a simple prototype of your idea. Remember that it doesn't need to look exactly like your idea looks in your mind. The important thing is that you can use your model to describe to someone else the most important parts of your design.

3 GET FEEDBACK

Share your model with a friend or an adult you trust and ask them what they think. You learned in the previous chapter what to do with the feedback you get. Make notes in your notebook using the same kind of page. Make a sketch of the prototype you built, like you learned before, so you remember which version you shared.

4 IMPROVE AND REPEAT

You're already a pro at this step. Use the things people told you to improve your solution and make a new model. Share it for feedback, take notes, and improve your solution one more time.

NAME YOUR SOLUTION

In the final box at the bottom of the page, draw the last version of your model. Now it's time to give it a name! What do you call your solution? Write the name next to the last box.

YOUR CITIZEN'S IRRESISTIBLE FUTURE

STORIES ARE THE most powerful when they are about people. Explaining how your solution works is great, but telling that story from the point of view of your citizen will make it even more personal and will help you make sure you are designing a future that your citizen will want to talk about!

PREPARATION

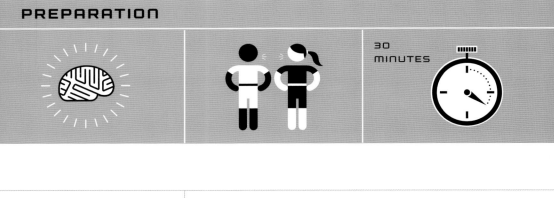

30 MINUTES

▶ WHAT YOU WILL NEED

▶ PREPARE YOURSELF

Before you get started, go back through your notes from this challenge and remind yourself of your citizen and his or her problem, your "what-if" question, and the solution you created.

1 · LET'S GO TO THE FUTURE

We're going to go to the future for this activity, imagining the day when you send your engineering design to City X and it is produced and delivered to your citizen. That will be an exciting day! You are making his or her irresistible future come true.

2 · PRETEND YOU ARE YOUR CITIZEN

When you tell the story of your solution, pretend you are your citizen. It doesn't matter if your citizen is a boy or a girl, young or old. It's good to imagine we are someone else to better understand the things we make. Think about what your citizen is like and how he or she might talk and move. Imagine the rest of your citizen's life and think of details! What does he or she do? What is the family like?

Become your citizen when you tell the story.

3 · TELL YOUR CITIZEN'S STORY

You already know the message your citizen communicated in user research. Now you have created a solution that can be held in his or her hands. Remember the three-act story method we learned to help you think about the different things you might want to share.

How has your (remember, you are your citizen!) life changed since you received your solution, and how do you use it in City X?

Write your story down or tell it to a friend or family member. It's just important that you share it so the world can know your genius.

CONGRATULATIONS

You have helped create an irresistible future for **environment** in City X.

THE
IRRESISTIBLE
FUTURES
AGENCY

3 DESIGN THE FUTURE OF COMMUNICATION

THE COMMUNICATION CHALLENGE is all about how we stay connected to the people in our lives. We talk to our friends, we share exciting news with our families, and we also use communication to learn, to run businesses, and to share important information with the public. Think about all of the ways you communicate now. Maybe you use a phone, write letters, send email or text messages, and of course you talk to people face to face! Imagine how these ways of communicating could be different on another planet. How will you help design the future of communication that helps the citizens of City X stay connected to people in their own city and also communicate with their friends and family on Earth? The citizens of City X have asked you, the Irresistible Futures agent, to think about three main things when designing the future of communication:

ELEMENT 1: MEDIUM

The medium of communication means the way we communicate, like talking out loud or writing. Usually new mediums of communication help us communicate more clearly, more quickly, or more cheaply. **How will you help the citizens of City X communicate better in their new world?**

ELEMENT 2: PRESENCE

One of the big challenges in City X is being so far away. An important part of communication is being present—standing next to someone, being able to touch them and feel their emotions. **How will you help the citizens of City X feel connected and present with loved ones far away?**

ELEMENT 3: LANGUAGE

The citizens of City X come from every part of Earth. They speak many languages but are all living together in one place, and they have a vision for a future that works for everyone. **How will you help the citizens of City X have a future where language is not a barrier to communication?**

EXPLORE ╌╌╌ ◆ ╌╌╌ ACTIVITY

THE "WHAT'S IN MY HEAD?" GAME

TO EXPLORE WHAT communication really means, imagine all the ways you use to communicate with other people. You talk, you use your hands, you make faces—everything we do when we communicate with others is part of making our ideas understood.

What if you had to communicate something complicated but could only use certain kinds of communication? In this activity we will try to get someone to understand what is in our head.

PREPARATION

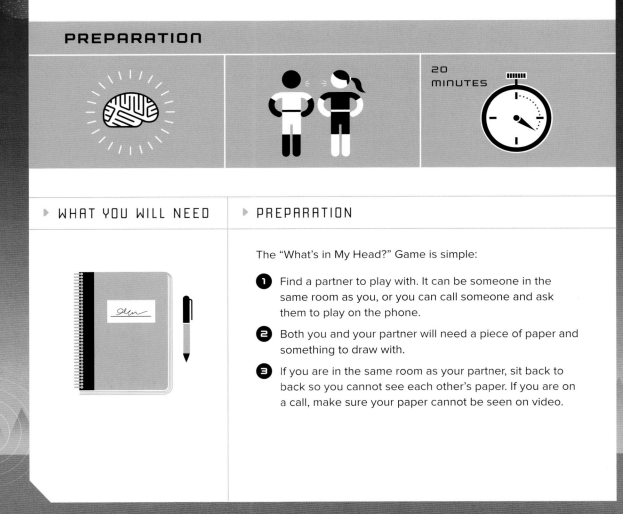

```
20
MINUTES
```

▶ WHAT YOU WILL NEED

▶ PREPARATION

The "What's in My Head?" Game is simple:

1 Find a partner to play with. It can be someone in the same room as you, or you can call someone and ask them to play on the phone.

2 Both you and your partner will need a piece of paper and something to draw with.

3 If you are in the same room as your partner, sit back to back so you cannot see each other's paper. If you are on a call, make sure your paper cannot be seen on video.

1 DRAW A PICTURE ON YOUR PAPER

Start by drawing a picture of your own. It can be anything you want, but use basic shapes (like squares, triangles, circles, stars, and hearts) to draw it. Have fun and be creative!

▶ **Make sure you don't show your partner what you are drawing!**

2 DESCRIBE YOUR PICTURE TO YOUR PARTNER

Now it's your partner's turn! Tell them they need to draw the picture you created, but they cannot see it. You can only describe it to them.

▶ **You can only use basic shape words to describe your picture.**

Draw a square. Then put 8 smaller squares on it. Add a vertical rectangle in the middle. Put a triangle on top.

3 COMPARE

How did your partner's drawing look? Was it the same as yours? How was it different?

Look at the pictures you and your partner created. Keep them safe in your notebook.

REFLECT

Communication is hard when we cannot use all the ways of communicating that we know.

How did you feel when you and your partner were communicating about your picture?

What did you learn about communication that you didn't know before?

USER RESEARCH: LETTER WRITING

HOW DO YOU think the citizens of City X feel about the future of communication? There are so many people in City X who all have different experiences and perspectives.

Because the citizens of City X come from different cultures, speak different languages, and have very different ways of communicating, we chose a user research method that would allow them to share a lot of details about their points of view. We started a letter-writing campaign, which means we invited anyone in City X to write a letter about their thoughts on communication and how to create a future where the communication challenge is solved. A summary of what we learned is below, along with excerpts from the letters written by five of the citizens of City X.

RESULTS

253 CITIZENS
WROTE LETTERS TO SHARE WITH THE IRRESISTIBLE FUTURES USER-RESEARCH TEAM.

6 LANGUAGES
WERE USED TO WRITE THE LETTERS.

LETTER	ゲヘヰꝏ
письмо	לעקרול
കത്ത്	ص خسين

60% OF THE LETTERS
MENTIONED MISSING FAMILY AND FRIENDS BACK ON EARTH.

LETTER WRITING

Letter writing is a form of user research that is good for learning a lot about how someone feels. It takes more time for a person to write a letter, but they can also share a lot more information about their perspective on a problem and a lot more information about what they care about for the future. Letter writing is often used when people want to share opinions with leaders and is especially useful when a problem is very emotional or difficult to manage.

Letter writing is good for

1. Sharing a lot of detail about feelings and opinions

2. Challenges that are emotional or complicated

3. User research that is about more than a simple choice between a few things

USER RESEARCH: CITIZEN PERSPECTIVES

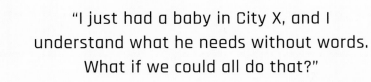

NEETA

"I just had a baby in City X, and I understand what he needs without words. What if we could all do that?"

LAURITA

"My husband works on one of the ships in orbit, so I don't get to see him much."

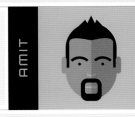

SASHA

"I want everyone in City X to have a voice in creating the future of our city."

AMIT

"People in City X speak so many languages. How can we communicate with each other?"

AHMED

"I didn't like phones and apps on Earth. Can't we communicate without looking at screens?"

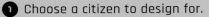

WHICH CITIZEN OF CITY X WILL YOU DESIGN FOR?

As an Irresistible Futures agent, you will design a solution for one of these City X citizens. Who will it be?

❶ Choose a citizen to design for.

❷ How do you think your citizen is feeling? Choose from some of the words to the right or come up with your own.

AWKWARD	CRANKY
HELPLESS	WORRIED
OUTRAGED	WISHFUL
UNHAPPY	ANNOYED

SYNTHESIZE — ACTIVITY

DRAW A PROBLEM MAP

WHEN WE TRY to **understand** complicated problems, it can be helpful to make a map of the challenge we want to solve. In this exercise we will practice a way to organize the information we have learned and use it to make our "what-if" statement for the future of City X.

PREPARATION

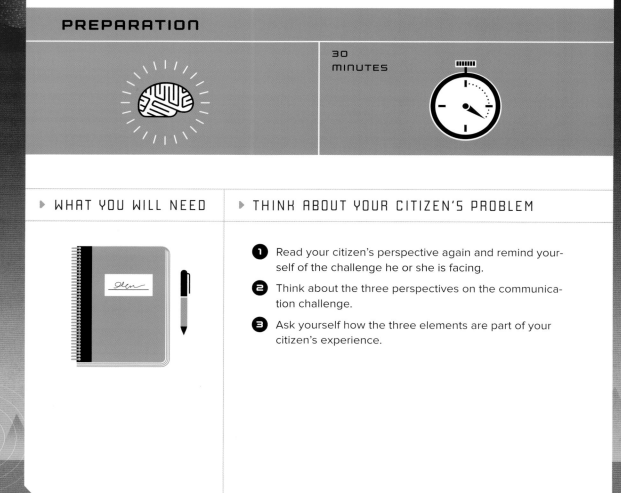

30 MINUTES

▸ WHAT YOU WILL NEED

▸ THINK ABOUT YOUR CITIZEN'S PROBLEM

1 Read your citizen's perspective again and remind yourself of the challenge he or she is facing.

2 Think about the three perspectives on the communication challenge.

3 Ask yourself how the three elements are part of your citizen's experience.

1 STATE THE PROBLEM

Begin with a blank page in your notebook. Write your citizen's problem in the center of the paper and put a square around it.

2 THINK ABOUT WHAT CAUSES THE PROBLEM

Above that box, think of what causes the problem. What makes it happen? Write as many reasons as you can think of and put a circle around each one with a line to the top of the box.

▶ **If you're having trouble thinking of causes, try playing the Why Game that you learned in the previous chapter!**

3 THINK ABOUT THE EFFECT OF THE PROBLEM

Below the box, now think about the effects of the problem:

What is the result in the life of your citizen?

How does the problem change his or her days and make life hard?

Why is it challenging?

Write as many reasons as you can think of and put a circle around each one with a line to the bottom of the box.

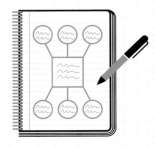

WRITE YOUR "WHAT-IF..." QUESTION

Turn your citizen's problem into a possibility. With all the new knowledge you have gained, write your own "what-if" question to share the possibility you see for the future of communication in City X.

CASE STUDY

INNOVATION BY ACCIDENT

HAVE YOU EVER wondered how people come up with new ideas? Sometimes it feels like all the ideas that could possibly be thought have already been thought by someone.

▸ WHERE DO WE FIND NEW IDEAS?

Throughout history, people have often tried to solve problems by thinking about the same paths others have taken or about what we "know" from our studies or people around us. Sometimes we forget that there is a whole universe of unexplained and unknown things, and the answers to our questions can surprise us.

▸ ACCIDENTAL INNOVATION

Accidents can actually make the best innovations! Accidents can come in a lot of forms—like when you try to do something and it turns out completely wrong, or when something unexpected happens and you find a new path you never knew existed. In this case study we'll learn about how accidents made possible three things everybody loves: being healthy, playing with clay, and eating cake.

THINK ABOUT IT

What was the last time you had to solve a hard problem? What did you do? Did you ask someone for help? Did you look it up on the internet? Or did you come up with a completely new way to solve your problem, one that nobody had ever done before?

CASE STUDY /// PENICILLIN

Penicillin is one of the most important discoveries in medicine in the last century. It is a medicine called an antibiotic, which means it can kill bacteria that make people sick. It was actually the first antibiotic ever made, and it has treated millions of people who might have died without it. But the discovery was an accident!

The scientist who discovered penicillin was actually researching a way to kill a different kind of germ that makes us sick, and he decided to leave his lab for a two-week vacation. He left a dish that had some bacteria growing in it on the counter and a little bit of mold floating in the air landed on it.

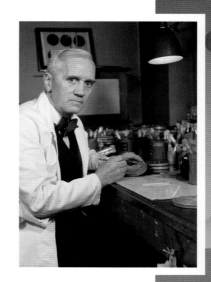

When he came back two weeks later, he was surprised to see that the mold was growing and the bacteria in the dish were dying. Eureka! The mold that had been floating in the air turned out to be a powerful antibiotic!

He never intended to find a treatment for so many bacterial illnesses that day, but he did because of an accident! Imagine how the world might be different today if he had remembered to put away that dish before he left!

CASE STUDY /// PLAY-DOH

Have you ever played with modeling clay like Play-Doh? The toy that everyone loves to squish and shape and bend was never supposed to be a toy. The company that invented it was actually trying to make a wallpaper cleaner! Their product never succeeded as a cleaner, but someone happened to see it one day and thought it had potential as a completely different product—as a toy. They added some nice coloring and a little scent, and the path of their product changed the course of many childhoods, all because of an accidental innovation!

CASE STUDY /// THE CAKE THAT FELL ON THE FLOOR

Massimo Bottura is one of the best chefs in the world, and the restaurant he runs in Italy is one of the best in the world, too. Perhaps the most famous dish they serve at the restaurant is called "Oops! I dropped the lemon tart." It looks just like it sounds—like a cake that someone dropped on the floor!

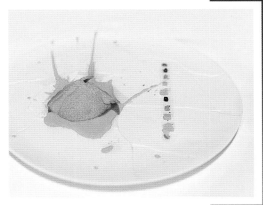

The innovation happened when one of the other chefs in the kitchen made a tart and accidentally dropped the plate. The tart broke and splattered on the plate. But instead of getting upset and replacing it, Bottura decided that it was perfect. Mistakes happen, and that is okay.

The dish is something people have now fallen in love with, and the story is one everyone can relate to.

We all make mistakes and it doesn't matter! Let's just hope the chefs in his kitchen don't start dropping everything!

TAKEAWAY

Mistakes are a part of learning and a part of life. Sometimes they help us find ideas and solutions that we never would have thought of before.

IMAGINE ———————— ACTIVITY

SCRAMBLED IMAGINATION

WARNING! COMMUNICATIONS HAVE BEEN SCRAMBLED!

YOUR CITY X citizen received a solution from another Irresistible Futures Engineer, but the communications were scrambled on the way to the new planet and parts of the message didn't make it through.

Could this be an accident that will bring about a new innovation and a new solution?

PREPARATION

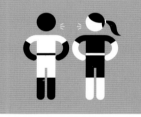

20 MINUTES

▶ WHAT YOU WILL NEED	▶ GET READY

Number your notebook page with 1 to 10.

The scrambled communication is on the next page. But there are several words missing! The citizens think they know what kind of words were supposed to be in the spaces, but they don't know what they were.

Remember two of the important rules for imagination are

1 Build on the ideas of others!

2 Wild ideas are great.

It's up to you to help turn this accident into a great idea!

1 FILL IN THE BLANKS

▶ **Don't read the communication just yet!** First we're going to choose some words to fill in the blanks.

You made a list of 1 to 10 in your notebook. Next to each number, write the type of word that is listed below. Whatever comes into your head, write that in your notebook next to that number.

1. A KIND OF MACHINE
2. A WAY YOU COMMUNICATE WITH WORDS
3. AN ACTION (SOMETHING PEOPLE DO WITH THEIR BODIES)
4. SOMETHING FAMILIES DO
5. YOUR FAVORITE ANIMAL
6. YOUR FAVORITE SHAPE
7. SOMETHING YOU SHARE
8. A FAMILY MEMBER
9. A FEELING
10. A NUMBER

2 READ THE NEW COMMUNICATION

Now read the scrambled communication, using the words from your list in each blank. Where you see (1) in the communication, put the word you wrote next to 1 on your paper. Do that for each number.

SCRAMBLED COMMUNICATION

I have designed a solution to help solve your communication problem, and I hope it works well for you!

It is a _____ **①** that makes _____ **②** into _____ **③**, which should help all of your friends and family _____ **④** with each other, even when you are far away. It looks like a _____ **⑤** but is made out of _____ **⑥**, and when you blow into it, it sends _____ **⑦** to your _____ **⑧** in 5 minutes.

You will feel _____ **⑨** when you use it. You should make _____ **⑩** so that you can share it with all of your friends and family!

YOUR IDEA IS READY

Does it sound like a great idea? Like a silly idea? Either way, it's okay! Remember, accidents and wild ideas are both great ways to make new solutions come true.

This is the solution you will create for your City X citizen. You can change things about it later, when you get feedback and improve it.

CREATE  ACTIVITY

BLUEPRINT YOUR IDEA

YOU'VE GOT A wild idea! Now it is time to turn it into reality!

When we take an idea from our head and bring it into the real world, it can be difficult to explain it exactly to another person. Imagine your dream house or all the parts of something like a telephone or a car, and then ask yourself how you would begin to tell someone how to make that.

This is where blueprinting comes in. A blueprint is a sketch or a model that you draw that includes all the parts of your idea. It usually has a few parts: basic shapes and outlines of the object, measurements to help someone understand how big it is, and labels to describe any parts that might not be clear.

PREPARATION

30 MINUTES

▸ **WHAT YOU WILL NEED**

▸ **PREPARATION**

1 Draw a line down the center of your page.

2 On the left side, make three boxes. Label the first one "Front." Label the second one "Side." Label the third one "Top."

PRACTICE

Let's try to make a simple blueprint first. Mario has a favorite yellow stuffed bear. How would we make a blueprint of the bear? **(A)**

First close your eyes and think about what the object looks like. Think about it from the front, from the side, and from the top. **(B)**

Each time you think about a new direction, draw what you see. Draw the basic shapes. It doesn't need to be exact! **(C)**

Then add notes like the size of the object or what certain parts do. **(D)**

BLUEPRINT YOUR SOLUTION

Now it's time to try your own! Let's make a blueprint of the wild solution you imagined for your City X citizen.

1. Reread the scrambled transmission and, as you're reading it, try to picture it in your head! What does your solution look like? What does it look like from the front, from the side, and from the top?

2. Make a sketch of your solution from all three perspectives.

3. Add labels for size and for the parts you want to explain.

IMPROVE AND REPEAT

You've gotten good at this already!

1. Share your blueprint with someone you trust and ask them for feedback as you explain it.

2. Make notes about things they like, things they don't like, and questions they ask.

3. Repeat steps 1 and 2!

What did you learn and how will you improve your idea? Write down at least two things in your notebook that you will change about your idea to make it stronger—and remember to thank the people who you talked to!

NAME YOUR SOLUTION

In the final box at the bottom of the page, draw the last version of your model. Now it's time to give it a name! What do you call your solution? Write the name next to the last box.

A.

B.

C.

D.

STORYBOARD

NOW IT'S TIME to share you solution and help people understand how it will help them and how they will use it. One method for this is making a **storyboard**.

A storyboard is a series of drawings that explains parts of the solution's story. Usually when you make a storyboard, you include people in the drawing and show how they are feeling and what they are doing. This helps make someone else feel like they are part of your story.

But what if I can't draw?

Everyone can make stick figures! Storyboards don't need to be complicated and in fact, research has shown that simple drawings like stick figures actually work better to share information and ideas. Because they do not look like anyone, they could look like everyone! So it is easy for some-one to imagine themselves in your drawing.

PREPARATION

20
MINUTES

▸ **WHAT YOU WILL NEED**

▸ **PREPARATION**

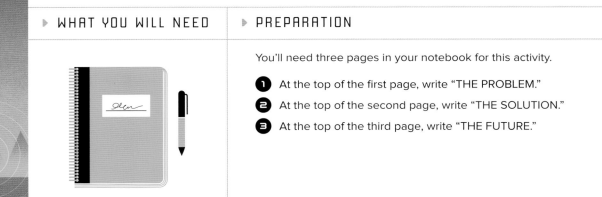

You'll need three pages in your notebook for this activity.

1 At the top of the first page, write "THE PROBLEM."

2 At the top of the second page, write "THE SOLUTION."

3 At the top of the third page, write "THE FUTURE."

1 DRAW THE PROBLEM

On the first page, draw your City X citizen experiencing his or her problem. What is your citizen doing? What is he or she feeling? Remember to show the emotions in the drawing!

2 DRAW THE SOLUTION

On the next page, now draw your City X citizen using your solution. What will it look like and feel like to use it?

3 DRAW THE FUTURE

What is the irresistible future you are creating for your City X citizen by making this solution? What will the future look like, now that your solution exists? How will life be different? Draw the vision of the future that your solution will help to make real.

Use these storyboards to help share your story with others. Explain what is in each picture and share your vision with the world.

CONGRATULATIONS

You have helped create an irresistible future for **communication** in City X.

THE
IRRESISTIBLE
FUTURES
AGENCY

4 DESIGN THE FUTURE OF FOOD

EVERYBODY LOVES FOOD! Food is a very important part of our lives. It keeps our bodies healthy and strong, it connects us with people in our lives, and it also represents our culture and our history. On Earth, a lot of our food is grown on farms. We eat animals and plants, but we also process the things we grow to make new types of foods. Everybody needs different kinds of food and likes different kinds of food, and some people have allergies to foods too. In City X the citizens don't have big farms or factories to make food, but they need to feed a big group of people who have all sorts of needs to stay healthy. How can you help design the future of food for City X?

The citizens of City X have asked you, the Irresistible Futures agent, to think about three main things when designing the future of food:

ELEMENT 1: AGRICULTURE

Have you ever seen a farm with animals and food growing in the ground? That's agriculture. The land in City X is different, and the citizens don't know which animals and plants are safe to eat on their new home world. **How will you help the citizens of City X safely produce food?**

ELEMENT 2: NUTRITION

A balanced diet is important for health. Everybody is unique though. We all need to eat different kinds of foods and in different amounts to keep us strong. **How will you help the citizens of City X provide the right nutrition to every person on their new home world?**

ELEMENT 3: POPULATION

Just like on Earth, the population of City X will soon be growing very quickly. The food supplies and sources will need to keep up to feed the growing city on our new planet. **How will you help the citizens of City X produce enough healthy food for everyone right when they need it?**

EXPLORE  ACTIVITY

MAKE AN EMPATHY WEB

UNDERSTANDING THE CHALLENGE of food is actually sort of easy! We all know what it is like to be hungry, to eat things we don't like, or to be far away from our houses and eating something we aren't used to. Maybe you even know what it's like to eat something that made you sick, or you need to eat some special food to stay healthy. In this activity we are going to think about those experiences a little bit more.

PREPARATION

30 MINUTES

▶ WHAT YOU WILL NEED

▶ THINK ABOUT THE FOOD CHALLENGE

In the last challenge we learned how to make a problem map, thinking about the causes and effects of a problem. In the food challenge, we are going to practice this skill but in a little different way.

Since we all understand at least a little bit what the food challenge might be like in City X, we're going to make an empathy web. It's sort of like a problem map, but about feelings!

1 PICK A PROBLEM YOU HAVE EXPERIENCED

Think about the food in your life. Maybe food at home, food at school, food on vacation, or food at a friend's house. What is a problem you have experienced with food?

Just like in the last challenge, write this problem you've experienced in the center of your notebook page and draw a box around it.

Now draw four lines from each corner of your box and label them like in this picture. Your page should look like this.

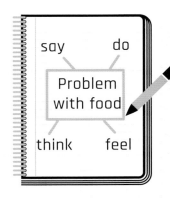

2 THINK ABOUT THE EXPERIENCE

Close your eyes and think about the problem you experienced with food. What was it like?

Think about four things:

1. What did you say?
2. What did you do?
3. What did you think?
4. What did you feel?

3 COMPLETE YOUR WEB

In the four corners of your map, write the things you felt, thought, did, and said when you were experiencing this problem. By doing this, we understand a little better what it is like for someone to be going through a food challenge.

REFLECT

In your notebook, write down three things you learned about food challenges that you didn't think about before.

USER RESEARCH: WORD ON THE STREET

FOOD IS A wonderful thing. It helps us to be healthy and strong, makes us happy, and connects people. Think about the first thing you often do with new people: You share a meal!

Since food is something everyone is always happy to talk about, the Irresistible Futures research team went to the streets of City X to ask people their opinions about the future of food in their city. Using a few simple questions that anyone would be able to answer easily, they made people comfortable and got them talking about their own ideas and visions for the future. Below you will find the most important pieces of information the research team learned, along with thoughts that five citizens agreed to have shared with you.

RESULTS

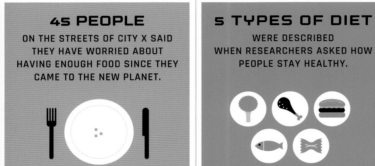

45 PEOPLE
ON THE STREETS OF CITY X SAID THEY HAVE WORRIED ABOUT HAVING ENOUGH FOOD SINCE THEY CAME TO THE NEW PLANET.

5 TYPES OF DIET
WERE DESCRIBED WHEN RESEARCHERS ASKED HOW PEOPLE STAY HEALTHY.

50 PERCENT
OF THE PEOPLE WE TALKED TO SAID THEY ARE THINKING ABOUT TRYING TO GROW THEIR OWN FOOD IN THE NEXT YEAR.

WORD ON THE STREET

When you want to learn what people think in an informal way, **word on the street** is a great type of user research. For this kind of research, you think of a few simple questions to ask about a topic that is easy to think about. Then you go out on the street and ask people you see if you could ask them a couple questions for some research you are doing. A lot of people might walk by because they have places to go, but the ones who stop will be happy to talk with you.

Word on the street is good for

1. Simple questions about easy topics

2. Learning the experiences of others in an informal way

3. Research in a place where you feel safe and comfortable

USER RESEARCH: CITIZEN PERSPECTIVES

AGUSTIN — "The days in City X can be quite short, so there isn't enough light to grow our crops."

SAIRA — "Everyone in my family eats a different diet, and I want to keep them all healthy."

ZAWADI — "We need to think about four generations in the future, when the population has grown many times."

TIAN-YI — "I really miss food from Earth that we can't make here."

ANURADHA — "How can we grow just the right amount of food for our city? No hunger, no waste!"

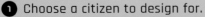

WHICH CITIZEN OF CITY X WILL YOU DESIGN FOR?

As an Irresistible Futures agent, you will design a solution for one of these City X citizens. Who will it be?

1 Choose a citizen to design for.

2 How do you think your citizen is feeling? Choose from some of the words to the right or come up with your own.

THANKFUL	NERVOUS
SCARED	KIND
GRUMPY	IMPATIENT
GENEROUS	MEAN

SYNTHESIZE   ACTIVITY

THE FOUR P'S

WE'VE LEARNED A LOT about the food challenge so far. Now let's take some time to synthesize— to make sense of our knowledge and think carefully about our citizen's problem.

In this exercise we are going to upgrade our skills as engineers and start asking deeper questions to understand challenges even more. We will be asking four questions about the problem our citizen is experiencing.

PREPARATION

30 MINUTES

▶ WHAT YOU WILL NEED

▶ PREPARE YOUR ENGINEER NOTEBOOK

Start a new page of your notebook and divide it into four sections. Label the sections

 Parts

 Patterns

 Problems

 People

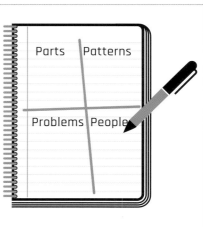

1 UNDERSTAND THE COMPONENTS

Parts, patterns, problems, and people are what we call "components" of a challenge. They're the smaller bits that a challenge is made up of. Every challenge has these.

Parts are the *things* that are involved in a challenge: the objects, the ideas, the structures. Parts could be things like dirt, plants, and the Sun (for an environment challenge) or vehicles, fuel, and distances (for the transportation challenge).

Patterns are the behaviors that are involved in a challenge. This one is a little harder to think about. Let's use the environment challenge as an example again. A pattern in the environment challenge would be "people throwing away recyclable plastic" or "cars polluting the air." These are behaviors or things that happen over and over and create challenges.

Problems are the things that are really hard to solve. For example, a problem in the environment challenge is how we can store energy that comes from the Sun. It needs a lot of research and technology to do it.

People are the easy part. They are all the individuals like you and like the City X citizens who are involved in a challenge. For example, in the environment challenge, the people might be farmers, mayors, truck drivers, and animals. (Animals can count as people too!)

2 WHAT ARE THE COMPONENTS OF YOUR CITIZEN'S CHALLENGE?

Now think about your citizen's challenge and make a list of the components in your notebook. Think carefully about each of these, so you can understand the challenge they are facing even better.

3 WHAT SEEM LIKE THE BEST COMPONENTS TO SOLVE?

Look over your four P's and decide which one or two seem like the best components for you to solve. You can choose one that you're most interested in or, if you feel adventurous, pick one you think will test you!

WRITE YOUR "WHAT-IF..." QUESTION

Turn your citizen's problem into a possibility. With all the new knowledge you have gained, write your own "what-if" question to share the possibility you see for the future of food in City X.

BUILDING OUR NEW HOME WORLD

THE IDEA OF humans leaving Earth and settling City X might seem like something from a science fiction future, but it is actually not so far from reality! There are people working right now to explore deep space and help humans become an interplanetary species. You might even someday have a job on another planet!

▸ WHY LEAVE EARTH?

Humans have always lived on just one planet: Earth. However, as our population grows, we know that our planet only has a limited amount of natural resources and space to support life. Most research shows that the Earth can support about 10 billion humans. Do you know how many people live on the Earth today?

Even if we don't leave Earth to actually live on another planet, we may need to look to other planets to find raw materials and resources that help sustain our life here.

▸ WHY IS LEAVING EARTH HARD?

Leaving Earth is very difficult! First, space is extremely large. With the technology available for space travel at the time this was written, just traveling to the Moon takes three days. But the closest solar system is more than 100 million times farther away!

Speed // One engineering challenge for space exploration is finding new types of propulsion. Propulsion is what makes something move. On your bike, your feet give propulsion. In a car, it is the engine that gives propulsion. To explore space, we need to find faster kinds of propulsion for our spacecraft.

Cargo // It is hard to carry things with us when we go to space. Everything we put into a spacecraft when it launches makes it heavier and slower. So another engineering challenge for space exploration is making the things we need in space, instead of taking them with us.

Health // Long space travel is difficult for human health. Imagine if you were in space for even three months, and could not eat your favorite foods or see a doctor if you were sick. How would you get food if you could not go to the supermarket? Keeping humans healthy in space is one big engineering challenge for space exploration.

▸ 3D PRINTING

Just like in City X, 3D printing is one of the technologies that will likely be used by humans to explore the universe. 3D printing is a way to make the things we need right where we need them, just by sending designs to a printer.

CASE STUDY (CONTINUED)

BUILDING OUR NEW HOME WORLD

CASE STUDY /// MADE IN SPACE

▸ WHAT IF WE COULD MAKE THINGS IN SPACE?

Made In Space is the company that created the first manufacturing facility in space. They started working in 2010, inspired by the idea of helping humans leave Earth to settle new planets. Made In Space invented the first 3D printer that worked in zero gravity, and in 2014 they produced the first object ever to be made off of Earth: a wrench that an astronaut needed on the International Space Station. They did not need to send a wrench on a spacecraft, they just emailed it to him as a design and he printed it on the 3D printer in space. Many things have now been made in space, and the technology is continuing to get better.

Making a wrench was the beginning, but what about building big structures we might need for living or working in space? Their Archinaut project is an experiment in building humanity's first off-Earth megastructures. The first challenge is to build a robotic 3D printer arm that orbits the Earth, building as it goes. It will create a satellite that is 1 kilometer (0.6 mi) wide!

While Made In Space is creating new ways of building in space, they are also helping humanity imagine new kinds of propulsion to explore our universe. Their RAMA project is one idea. The experiment would send a 3D printer to land on an asteroid. When it lands, the printer would build a spacecraft around the asteroid, and it would use the propulsion of the asteroid to move! Small engines could gently change the path of the asteroid to make our new spacecraft go wherever we want it to.

REFLECT

If you could build a megastructure in space, what would you want to build? What features would you want it to have?

CASE STUDY /// NASA

As humans venture deeper into space, staying healthy is a challenge. Thinking about manned missions to Mars, NASA has begun researching new ways of producing food for these voyages. One of their experiments was to build a 3D printer that created food for astronauts. Instead of printing with plastic or metal, these printers would print with nutrients! This would allow each person on a spacecraft to create food that meets their own nutritional requirements, and the individual nutrients would have much longer storage life than prepared or dried food. The first prototype was to build a 3D printer that would make pizza!

If you had a 3D printer that would make you customized food, what would you want it to make? As an engineer, what are the things you would want it to be able to do?

TAKEAWAY

Sometimes the things that sound like science fiction are actually real! The world is changing faster than we think, so imagine your future without limits!

INTERCONNECTED CHALLENGES

A LOT OF the challenges facing City X are connected. Transportation has a lot to do with the environment, for example. And health has a lot to do with safety. Think about other challenges you might face in your own life. How many of them are connected to others?

In this activity we will come up with ideas to solve your citizen's problem in a way that helps us build connections between ideas and generate more great solutions.

PREPARATION

30
MINUTES

▶ **WHAT YOU WILL NEED**

▶ **PREPARE YOUR NOTEBOOK**

Maps, maps, maps! We've learned problem mapping and empathy mapping. Now we're going to make a new kind of map: a mind map.

Just like with the last two maps, we'll start by putting something right in the middle of the page. This time, write your "what-if" statement for your City X citizen.

1 START WITH FOUR IDEAS

What are four different ideas for how you could make your "what-if" question come true? Start by writing these four around your central question.

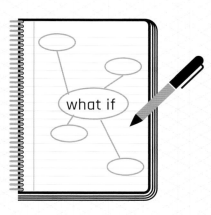

2 GO A STEP DEEPER

Now, for each of your four solutions, ask yourself, "Could this solution be used to solve any other challenge in City X?" What if you changed it just a little bit?

Around each solution, think of ways you could improve your idea so that it could be used to solve multiple challenges at once.

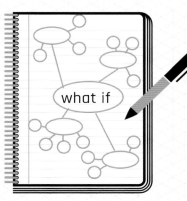

3 DRAW CONNECTIONS

Look over all of the ideas you have on the page. Draw lines between any ideas that are similar or maybe could be combined. Is there one that is the most exciting? Is there one that could solve the most problems at once?

CHOOSE YOUR FAVORITE IDEA

What new ideas did you come up with? Select your favorite idea and get ready to create!

CREATE ACTIVITY

CLAY MODELING

YOU HAVE A great solution in mind to solve your citizen's food challenge. Now let's bring that idea out of your brain and into the world!

We learned in the previous challenge about Innovation by Accident, and one of the accidents was Play-Doh! So why not get our hands a little dirty and use that accidental innovation to model your solution?

PREPARATION

45
MINUTES

▸ WHAT YOU WILL NEED

▸ PREPARATION

Make sure you start with a clean, dry area. If you don't have Play-Doh, any kind of modeling clay will work just fine!

1 BRING IT TO LIFE

Use the clay to create a model of your solution. The best part about using clay is that it's easy to make it look just how you want. You can mold it into almost any shape and use multiple colors to show what different parts are.

Did you know that engineers who make cars and other big machines often use clay as their first models, too? It's because of just this reason—it's so easy to make it look close to what you really envision.

2 SHARE IT WITH SOMEONE

Use your model to tell someone about your solution. Let them ask questions about your creation. Make sure you take notes the way you've been trained as an Irresistible Futures agent!

Here is a model of my solution. It is . . .

3 IMPROVE AND REPEAT

Go back and make changes to your model based on the feedback from others. Then share again and repeat!

After you've made your last version of the model, keep it safe—you'll need it later.

NAME YOUR SOLUTION

Now it's time to give it a name! What do you call your solution? Write the name next to the last box, on your improve and repeat page.

TV COMMERCIAL

WHEN ENGINEERS COME up with really good ideas, they want other people to know about them. Otherwise, nobody would know your brilliant solution exists! One of the most popular ways for designers and engineers to share their ideas is through a commercial, like you would see while you are watching a television show.

Commercials are short—only about 30 seconds long—and they highlight the most important features of your solution. They also make people feel something.

In this activity you will think about how you would convince someone to use your solution in just thirty seconds, in your very own commercial.

PREPARATION

30 MINUTES

▶ WHAT YOU WILL NEED

▶ PREPARATION

Keep you clay model handy for this activity. Commercials usually show people using a solution, so it's easy to understand how it is used and what it does. Your model will be perfect for this.

If you need a reminder about the important parts of a story, you can use the three-act story method from the first chapter to think about all the things you might want to share.

1 DECIDE WHO IS IN YOUR COMMERCIAL

You, as the inventor, could be sharing what you made. Or maybe you could be acting, pretending you are your City X citizen using your solution. Or maybe you ask a friend to be in your commercial with you, and you can show them what to do.

2 DECIDE THE MOST IMPORTANT THINGS TO SHARE

Your commercial will be only 30 seconds long, so think about the most important things to share. What do you want to make sure you tell? The name of your solution is probably important, and be sure to say what problem it solves and how it works.

3 DECIDE HOW YOU WANT SOMEONE TO FEEL

How do you want your commercial to make someone feel? Happy? Excited? Thoughtful?

4 WRITE YOUR COMMERCIAL

You can write a script for your commercial with the lines you'll say. Include lines for a friend too, if there is more than one person in your commercial. Think about what each person will say and make sure that you share the most important things and make people feel the way you want.

5 PERFORM YOUR COMMERCIAL

You can perform your commercial for friends or family—or even just for yourself! If you want to, ask an adult you trust to record your commercial so you can watch it later, just like on TV!

CONGRATULATIONS

You have helped create an irresistible future for **food** in City X.

THE
IRRESISTIBLE
FUTURES
AGENCY

5 DESIGN THE FUTURE OF HEALTH

BEING HEALTHY IS important to building a future that works for everyone. When we are sick or hurt, we can't go to school, we can't work, we can't spend time with our families, and we can't have fun! Staying healthy on Earth means eating good food, taking medicine when you need to, visiting your doctor for checkups, and taking time to relax and enjoy life. In City X the citizens don't have hospitals and clinics yet, and it is hard to get medicines sent to a new planet when they are needed. How could you help create a future for City X that considers all parts of the citizens' health?

The citizens of City X have asked you, the Irresistible Futures agent, to think about three main things when designing the future of health:

ELEMENT 1: PREVENTION

Our health is the strongest if we never get sick to begin with. We know how to avoid germs and infections and injuries on Earth, but in City X, nobody is prepared to protect themselves. **How will you help the citizens of City X prevent themselves from getting sick and hurt?**

ELEMENT 2: TREATMENT

When we do get sick, we want to get better quickly and without causing any more harm to ourselves now or later. A lot of treatments come from plants and chemicals that won't be available on the new planet. **How will you help the citizens of City X treat their illnesses?**

ELEMENT 3: EMOTIONAL

Sometimes it is easy to know when you are hurt or sick, like when you have a cut or your stomach feels bad. Other times our health is invisible, like when our feelings or our minds are hurting. **How will you help the citizens of City X keep these invisible parts healthy too?**

EXPLORE ◆ ACTIVITY

YOUR OWN LIFE

THE HEALTH CHALLENGE is one that almost anyone can understand. Humans get sick or hurt themselves quite often, and sometimes it can be very serious. In this activity, we will think about our own health and the health of our family and friends.

PREPARATION

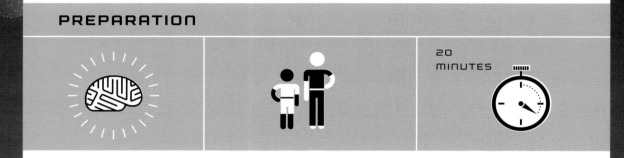

20
MINUTES

▶ WHAT YOU WILL NEED

▶ PREPARATION

To complete this activity you'll want to prepare your design notebook for some research. In the last challenge we learned about the different ways you experience challenges. We will practice this again as we think about health, but instead of thinking just about ourselves, we will ask how health problems affect other people, too.

1 Make your notebook page into three sections. Label them "Think," "Feel," and "Do."

2 Now, across the top, add two columns: "Me" and "You."

1 THINK ABOUT THE LAST TIME YOU HAD A HEALTH PROBLEM

Try to remember the last time you were hurt or sick. Do you remember what happened? In your notebook, under "Me," write or draw what you were thinking, what you were feeling, and what you were doing last time you were hurt or sick.

2 ASK AN ADULT OR FRIEND WHO WAS WITH YOU

For the second step, you'll need to talk to an adult or a friend who was with you when it happened. Maybe it is one of your parents, a teacher, or someone you were playing with. Ask them the same questions, but try to understand what it was like for *them* to experience your health problem.

3 RECORD YOUR RESEARCH

Write or draw what your partner tells you about what it was like when you were hurt or sick. Think about how their experience was different from yours. What were the emotions you felt and what were the emotions they felt?

REFLECT

In your notebook, write down three things you learned about health challenges that you didn't think about before.

USER RESEARCH: POINT OF SERVICE

IF YOU ASK a group of people how they stay healthy, chances are you will have many different answers. Everyone has their own activities and exercise routines, and everyone needs to keep their minds and bodies strong.

For this user research, the Irresistible Futures research team wanted people to already be thinking about health before they asked questions. So they went to the small health center in City X, where citizens can exercise and get basic health checkups from a nurse. The team chose this kind of research—going to the point of service—not just to learn what people think about health but to learn how health is already being protected in City X. Here are some of the results and the opinions shared by citizens there.

RESULTS

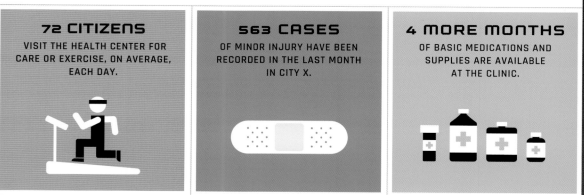

72 CITIZENS
VISIT THE HEALTH CENTER FOR CARE OR EXERCISE, ON AVERAGE, EACH DAY.

563 CASES
OF MINOR INJURY HAVE BEEN RECORDED IN THE LAST MONTH IN CITY X.

4 MORE MONTHS
OF BASIC MEDICATIONS AND SUPPLIES ARE AVAILABLE AT THE CLINIC.

POINT OF SERVICE

Going to the **point of service** is a great way to conduct research when you want to learn about a system or an experience that people are already having. Where would you go on Earth to learn about how we keep people healthy? Probably to the doctor's office or the hospital, where you can find the people who keep us healthy and the people who are experiencing health problems. When you are there, you can ask for all the data about a problem but also get a chance to see a problem in person and observe the way it works.

Point of service research is good for

1. Understanding a problem from different perspectives at one time

2. Getting data from other users who are not there when you are

3. Observing the interaction people have with a system

USER RESEARCH: CITIZEN PERSPECTIVES

YUKA

"I am at the health center because I cut myself, but what would happen if I got seriously hurt?"

"I love to explore nature outside City X. I want to keep myself safe when I do."

ASIM

LAILA

"I get sad because I have to stay inside a lot of the time in City X."

"My friend ate something he didn't know was poisonous and was sick for a week."

DARANA

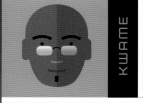

KWAME

"I coach a football team in City X and I don't want my players to get hurt."

WHICH CITIZEN OF CITY X WILL YOU DESIGN FOR?

As an Irresistible Futures agent, you will design a solution for one of these City X citizens. Who will it be?

1 Choose a citizen to design for.

2 How do you think your citizen is feeling? Choose from some of the words to the right or come up with your own.

SICK	PANICKED
PEACEFUL	IRRITATED
UNCERTAIN	TERRIFIED
HURT	VULNERABLE

SYNTHESIZE ——— ACTIVITY

THINK LIKE A DOCTOR

DOCTORS AND NURSES need to think carefully about health challenges every day. They have a big job: keeping everyone healthy. As you engineer solutions to health challenges in City X, it might help to think like a doctor! In this activity you will learn how to use a tool that doctors and nurses actually use to think carefully about their patients' health challenges, and you will use it for your City X citizen!

PREPARATION

30 MINUTES

▶ **WHAT YOU WILL NEED**

▶ **WHAT YOU NEED TO KNOW**

The tool you will learn in this activity is called the SBAR. Each letter of the name stands for a word that is an important part of solving the patient's problem.

A really important part of the SBAR is that all of the people caring for a patient know it. It ensures that everyone understands the problem completely and understands the plan for what they are going to do. To start, let's make sure we understand all of the words!

S stands for **situation**. The situation is a very simple, clear statement of the challenge.

B stands for **background**. The background is any information that is important to know in order to understand the situation.

A stands for **assessment**. The assessment is thinking carefully about the background and situation to make sure you understand the root cause of the problem.

R stands for **response**. The response is what you will do about the problem.

We'll prepare our notebook for careful thinking.

1 THINK ABOUT THE SITUATION AND BACKGROUND

This step is just about the facts.

Your City X citizen has told you about their challenge. In your notebook write down the situation and the background. Remember, the situation is a simple statement of the problem, and the background is any important and helpful information.

2 MAKE YOUR ASSESSMENT

When you make an assessment, your job is to think carefully about what you know and what options are and are not available. Think about your citizen's challenge. What is your assessment of the situation?

3 START YOUR RESPONSE

Let's think about all of your assessments. Do they point you in a certain direction? What do you think is the best thing to do next?

Start your response with your "what-if" question, turning a problem into a possibility!

EXAMPLE

Agustin's challenge:

PROBLEM
"The days in City X can be quite short, so there isn't enough light to grow our crops."

Situation:
not enough light to grow crops.

Background:
days are short, living on new planet far away, sunlight is weaker than on Earth, lots of people to feed, crops require 8 hours of light a day.

Assessment:
· Problem is very serious.
· Growing food is necessary in City X.
· We cannot make days longer.
· We cannot send food to City X because it is far away.
· We can find other ways to make food.
· We can find other ways to create energy.

POSSIBILITY
One of our agents suggested:
"What if we didn't need sunlight to create energy?"

WRITE YOUR "WHAT-IF..." QUESTION

Turn your citizen's problem into a possibility. With all the new knowledge you have gained, write your own "what-if" question to share the possibility you see for the future of health in City X.

THE WORLD'S YOUNGEST SPACE ENGINEER

IN THE FOOD challenge you met a company called Made In Space, which built the world's first zero-gravity 3D printer for the International Space Station. Made In Space was a partner in the beginning of the City X mission, and they wanted to help Irresistible Futures engineers understand that they really could design solutions that could be sent to space.

▶ YOUR CAREER SOMEDAY MIGHT NOT BE ON EARTH

Jason, the cofounder of Made In Space, wanted young engineers to know that when they think about their futures, it really is possible they could be working in space or even on another planet.

So Jason and the founders of City X launched a competition to find the world's youngest space engineer. One young person from Earth who was designing a solution to a challenge in City X would be selected to have their solution 3D printed by a real astronaut *in space* on the International Space Station.

▶ THE WORLD'S YOUNGEST SPACE ENGINEER

James was 9 years old when he was selected by Made In Space to become the world's youngest space engineer. The designs for his City X solution were sent to space and manufactured using the 3D printer on the International Space Station.

CASE STUDY /// JAMES AND MIGUEL

▶ HEALTH CHALLENGES IN CITY X

James was designing a solution for Miguel, a citizen of City X who had fallen out of a tree and broken his arm.

Do you remember the lesson in the Engineer Briefing about personal problems and social problems?

James knew that he couldn't do anything to help Miguel with his broken arm; that was something he would need to go to the health center for. James understood that the problem Miguel shared was part of a bigger social problem about access to emergency care and how people could get treatment in a new city on a new planet.

▶ JAMES'S SOLUTION: THE HEALTH COASTER

James thought big about health and then thought carefully to understand how he could solve Miguel's problem in City X. He used all of the rules for imagination and designed a remarkable invention: the Health Coaster.

The Health Coaster is a universal treatment device that heals anything wrong with you. It considers all the parts of health that are important. James knew that going to the doctor sometimes takes a long time, and it is sometimes scary and stressful. So the health coaster has a massaging attachment to keep you calm and a candy dispenser just in case you get hungry. And the best part? It rides on a roller coaster track so that going to the doctor is *always fun*.

James's Health Coaster was manufactured in space, and you can see it here floating in front of the Earth. At 9 years old, James proved the future can be whatever we want to make it. It can be an irresistible future that solves problems in new ways and sends our ideas and ourselves to the stars.

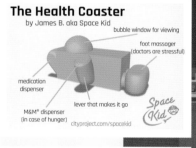

The Health Coaster
by James B. aka Space Kid

bubble window for viewing
foot massager (doctors are stressful)
medication dispenser
lever that makes it go
M&M® dispenser (in case of hunger)
cityproject.com/spacekid
Space Kid

TAKEAWAY

Maybe the job you have someday won't be on Earth. By learning to solve problems and think big today, you open a future of exciting possibilities.

IMAGINE · ACTIVITY

DESIGNING WITH CONSTRAINTS

WHEN WE DESIGN solutions, it's so much fun to think about a world where everything is possible, where we can come up with ideas that will work for everybody. But in reality, we live in a universe with constraints. Constraints are things that bring limits to what we create. A constraint could be as simple as running out of peanut butter when you make a sandwich (constraint: peanut butter supply is low!) or as complicated as the amount of medicine you can give someone safely in a hospital (constraint: too much medicine can make someone sicker).

It might seem like constraints could make things harder, but actually constraints make you so much more creative. When we have to find a solution even though there is a constraint, it makes us think bigger and more boldly as we try to solve our challenges.

PREPARATION

20 MINUTES

▶ WHAT YOU WILL NEED

▶ FLASH LEARNING

The Psychology of Constraint

Remember in the very first challenge, the imagine exercise was just about making a first mark? Making that first mark is so hard because your options are limitless! You could do anything! What if it's wrong? What if it could be better?

Being creative can be easier with constraints because your mind understands where it needs to focus its energy. It doesn't see a completely blank page and feel so scared!

NEW LAW PASSED IN CITY X

City X passed a new law this week that requires all new solutions engineered for the city to be usable by anyone, no matter their abilities or age.

- **People who move** around in different ways (for example, people who walk or people who use a wheelchair)
- **People who sense** (see, hear, feel) in different ways (for example, people who see with a guide dog or people who see with glasses)
- **People who learn** in different ways and at different speeds
- **People who communicate** in different ways, including languages, gestures, and thoughts

1 THINK ABOUT THE IMPLICATIONS

Implications are the result of something. If you have a constraint like a new law, the implications are what happens because of it.

How does the new law make you think differently as you imagine solutions?

Start by making a list in your design notebook of all of the types of abilities you might need to think about. What different abilities can you list? Consider how people think, how people feel, how people do things, and how people say things.

2 IMPROVE YOUR WHAT-IF QUESTION

Do you need to improve your "what-if" question? Sometimes constraints help us make a better question, which helps us imagine better solutions.

3 IMAGINE

Use whatever your favorite method is to imagine solutions to your citizen's challenge. Remember that your solutions need to respect the new law in City X! They must be accessible to everyone in the city.

CHOOSE YOUR FAVORITE IDEA

Before you continue, make sure your solution meets all the constraints:

1. Accessible to people of all ages
2. Accessible to people of all abilities

CREATE ACTIVITY

FEEDBACK FROM EVERYONE

WHEN WE DESIGN solutions, often we think about solutions that work for people just like us. It could be that we think about people who are the same age or who are from the same place or speak the same language. It could also be that we think about people who have the same abilities as we do. The previous activity helped us think about designing within a new constraint in City X, that all solutions must be usable by everyone in the city.

In this activity we will test our idea by building a prototype and getting feedback from people who are different from us.

PREPARATION

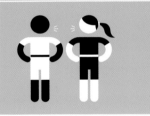

2 HOURS

▶ WHAT YOU WILL NEED

▶ CREATE A MODEL

By now you have learned how to create models in many different ways. You have learned sketches, blueprinting, clay models, and prototyping with things around the house.

Choose your favorite way of creating a model and create one for your solution.

Now that you have a model, it's time to test your idea with feedback from everyone. The goal of this activity is to understand how people who are different than you think about your solution.

1 MAKE AN IMPROVE AND REPEAT PAGE

Prepare your notebook for feedback with an Improve and Repeat page.

2 TELL SOMEONE DIFFERENT ABOUT YOUR SOLUTION

For this you might need to ask an adult you trust for help. As an engineer, it is important to talk to people you might not usually talk to. For this activity the people you talk to should be people of a different age, a different background, or different abilities.

Depending on what your solution is and which City X citizen you are designing for, there may be some people who can give you better feedback than others. But a good goal is to talk to at least one person you don't usually talk to who is older than you and one person who has abilities of any kind (look back at the previous activity for a reminder!) that are different than yours.

Tell them about your solution and listen carefully to their feedback. A good question to ask is "How could I make my solution better so that every person in a city could use it?" As always, write down the good things, the questions, and the changes you could make.

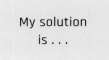

My solution is . . .

3 IMPROVE AND REPEAT

Make changes to your model based on the feedback. Share it with another person and make one final round of changes.

NAME YOUR SOLUTION

You've created a solution that works for everybody! At the bottom of your Improve and Repeat page, record your final version of the model. Now it's time to give it a name! What do you call your solution? Write the name next to the last box.

SHARE ACTIVITY

A POETIC SOLUTION

THERE ARE SO many ways to share our ideas with other people. But sometimes when we use a lot of words, it just gets confusing and people won't remember it. In this activity you will use just a small number of words to share your solution and the irresistible future it will create.

In this activity you will write a haiku about your solution. A haiku is a kind of poem with only three lines. Each line has a certain number of syllables: The first line has five syllables, the second line has seven syllables, and the third line has five syllables.

PREPARATION

30 MINUTES

▶ WHAT YOU WILL NEED

▶ FLASH LEARNING

What does poetry have to do with engineering? Sharing our ideas is one of the most important parts of designing solutions. If our goal is to create futures that work for everyone, that needs to be a future everyone can understand. We need to be careful and thoughtful about our words.

A great example is the story of the American President Abraham Lincoln giving the Gettysburg Address—it was one of the most famous speeches ever given and it lasted only three minutes. The newspapers of the day mostly ignored it. They talked instead about the ninety-minute speech that another speaker had given at the same event. But of course, history remembers Lincoln's three minutes of carefully chosen, powerful words that told the story he wanted to tell—a story everyone could understand.

1 COMPLETE A THREE-ACT STORY

Think about the solution you created for your citizen and complete a three-act story page to recall the problem, the irresistible future you wish to create, and the solution that will make it happen.

2 MAKE EACH ACT INTO ONE LINE OF YOUR POEM

For each act of the three-act story, write one line of the poem.

The first line is about the problem—
only five syllables!

The second line is about the future—
only seven syllables!

The last line is about the solution—
only five syllables!

A haiku does not need to rhyme. But it can, for an extra challenge!

3 DRAW A PICTURE TO GO WITH THE POEM

Draw a picture that goes with your poem and put them both on a page of your design notebook. Share your solution—and your short but powerful story—with the world.

Let's think about Agustin's challenge that we used as an example earlier. We might write a haiku that goes something like this:

Crops they do not grow,

So let's not need sunlight's glow,

Food that grows in dark.

CONGRATULATIONS

You have helped create an irresistible future for **health** in City X.

THE
IRRESISTIBLE
FUTURES
AGENCY

6 DESIGN THE FUTURE OF ENERGY

ENERGY POWERS ALL of the things in our lives. Energy makes our cars move, our lights turn on, and our factories run. We use energy to make breakfast and watch TV, and to launch ships into space. A lot of our energy on Earth comes from resources that we take out of our planet. But you remember from the Environment challenge that the citizens want to build City X in a way that protects the environment and makes everyone healthy. How will you help design a future of energy that will power all the things City X needs, will help humans travel long distances easily, and will use resources that will never run out?

The citizens of City X have asked you, the Irresistible Futures agent, to think about three main things when designing the future of energy:

ELEMENT 1: SUSTAINABILITY

One of the reasons humans need to explore other planets is because there is only a limited amount of resources on Earth. **How will you help the citizens of City X create power from resources that are clean and will not run out or will grow back when they use them?**

ELEMENT 2: STORAGE

Did you know that in just 1 hour on Earth, the energy that reaches the planet from the Sun is more than humans use in an entire year? We just don't have anywhere to store that much energy to use later! **How will you help the citizens of City X store energy from their sun?**

ELEMENT 3: DELIVERY

Just like on Earth, a lot of solar energy reaches the new planet. But only one part of the planet is sunny all the time, and it's not near City X. **Once the citizens have a way to store the energy, how will you help the citizens of City X deliver energy to the city and to ships in orbit?**

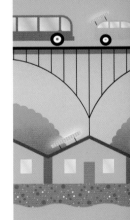

EXPLORE ACTIVITY

LIVE A DAY

WE DON'T THINK a lot about many of the things we use in our lives. How many times today did you think about where the water you drank came from or who cooked your food or who built your school?

In this activity, we are going to **explore** the energy we use each day by living an entire day without it!

PREPARATION

1 DAY

▶ WHAT YOU WILL NEED

▶ PREPARE YOURSELF

You will need permission for this activity because you are going to do something a little bit silly: **You will live an entire day without energy.** It is probably best to do this activity on a weekend or on a day when you don't need to go to school.

Plan ahead! Think about how you will do some things you normally do if you cannot use energy.

THINK ABOUT IT

Before you get started, think about all the ways you use energy every day. Ask an adult you trust to help and **make a complete list in your design notebook.**

1 GO ABOUT YOUR DAY

When your day starts, remind yourself that you have to live the entire day without using energy. Your friends or family might offer to help you or to use energy for you, but that would be cheating!

2 KEEP TRACK

Every time you find yourself needing to use energy, make a check mark next to that category in your notebook. If you find new ways that you didn't think of, add them to the list and keep track of those too.

3 FIND A DIFFERENT WAY

Every time you think about using energy, try to find another way to do what you need that doesn't use energy. Make a list of all the alternatives you found and also make a list of anything you needed to do that you absolutely could not find another way to accomplish.

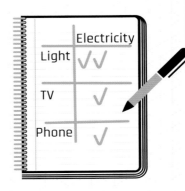

REFLECT

How hard was it to live a day without energy?

Think about your experience living without energy. It was probably hard, and you only did it for one day!

What new ideas did you get today when you were thinking about how to complete tasks that usually use energy?

USER RESEARCH: DATA ANALYSIS

ENERGY IS USED by everyone in City X, and there are many different kinds of energy used for different activities. There are many pieces of information we could collect about energy.

The Irresistible Futures research team has collected data from all of the people in City X to learn about what kind of energy they use, how much energy they use, what they use it for, and when they use it. It was a lot of information, so they used a powerful computer program to do data analysis. The program told us some important things, which you'll find below. The team asked some follow-up questions to several citizens as well, and their answers are here, too.

RESULTS

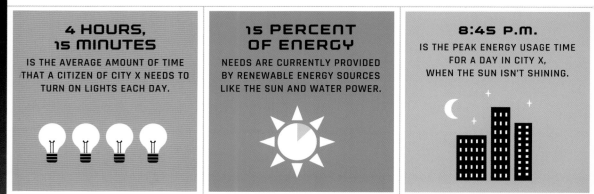

4 HOURS, 15 MINUTES
IS THE AVERAGE AMOUNT OF TIME THAT A CITIZEN OF CITY X NEEDS TO TURN ON LIGHTS EACH DAY.

15 PERCENT OF ENERGY
NEEDS ARE CURRENTLY PROVIDED BY RENEWABLE ENERGY SOURCES LIKE THE SUN AND WATER POWER.

8:45 P.M.
IS THE PEAK ENERGY USAGE TIME FOR A DAY IN CITY X, WHEN THE SUN ISN'T SHINING.

DATA ANALYSIS

Data is information that we get from different kinds of sources. For example, if you asked everyone in your family how old they are, you would write down a number for each one of them. Those numbers are data! When we have very big numbers and a lot of data, like when we collect information from everyone in a city, it's hard to make sense of those numbers and learn things from them. That's when **data analysis** is a really good tool for user research. We can put all the numbers and data into a computer program and learn important things about a problem.

Data analysis is good for

1. Very large sets of information that we need to understand

2. Information that is mostly numbers

3. Getting important insights into complicated problems

USER RESEARCH: CITIZEN PERSPECTIVES

EUNJOO

"The big batteries we brought to City X are almost used up."

"We want to keep exploring space but need a new kind of energy for our ships."

RODRIGO

MYRIAM

"There should be a law in City X requiring that energy does not pollute the environment."

"What if energy was so plentiful and clean, nobody had to pay for it?"

MUKUL

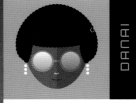

DANAI

"The winter here is very cold."

WHICH CITIZEN OF CITY X WILL YOU DESIGN FOR?

As an Irresistible Futures agent, you will design a solution for one of these City X citizens. Who will it be?

1 Choose a citizen to design for.

2 How do you think your citizen is feeling? Choose from some of the words to the right or come up with your own.

RELAXED	JOYFUL
ALARMED	CARING
PROUD	SKEPTICAL
LONELY	TROUBLED

SYNTHESIZE **ACTIVITY**

FIRST PRINCIPLES

WHEN WE THINK about complicated challenges, there are so many parts to consider. If someone asks you to "solve the energy problem," where would you even begin?

First principles thinking is a way of breaking down complicated things into their basic parts. This way of thinking helps identify the best things to improve or change or even find a whole new way of putting those parts together.

In this activity, you will use first principles thinking to break down your citizen's problem into its basic parts and then choose one of those parts to improve in order to design a solution.

PREPARATION

45 MINUTES

▶ **WHAT YOU WILL NEED**

▶ **PRACTICE**

To learn first principles thinking, let's start by thinking about a thing that we use, like a bicycle. **What are the basic parts of a bicycle?**

A metal frame, a seat, pedals, wheels, a chain, and gears. Oh, and our feet! We make a bicycle move using our feet. And we use it to move from one place to another.

Sometimes when we make the list, it is helpful to ask a couple extra questions, like "How does it work?" and "What need does it fill?" These questions help us think about other parts, like feet, and getting from one place to another.

Practice now, thinking about a book! What are the first principles of a book?

What are the parts?
Pages, words, pictures, hands, information, and stories.

1 UNDERSTAND FIRST PRINCIPLES FOR PROBLEMS

When we think about first principles for problems, it works in the same way. We start by thinking about all the parts of the problem. These parts can be physical things, like the seat and wheels of the bike, or activities that are important. Remember to ask yourself extra questions like "How does it work?" and "What need does it fill?" Let's do an example.

2 YOUR FIRST PRINCIPLES

Think about the problem your citizen is facing. What are the first principles of the problem? Since all of the citizens in this chapter face challenges with energy, you can start there! What are the first principles of energy? When you make your list, remember to think about the physical parts of energy, as well as how energy works and the need that it fills.

What is unique about your citizen's problem? What other first principles can you think about that other citizens might not be facing?

3 CHOOSE A FIRST PRINCIPLE TO FOCUS ON

The reason we use first principles thinking is so we can focus our energy on solving the parts of challenges that will make a big difference.

Look at your list of first principles. Choose one to focus on as you engineer a solution for your City X citizen.

EXAMPLE

Mario's challenge:

PROBLEM
"Could our homes and buildings be more friendly to the natural world?"

First Principles:
construction sites
heavy machines
big buildings
pollution
materials (concrete, wood, glass, chemicals)
plants
animals
habitats
places to live, places to work

WRITE YOUR "WHAT-IF..." QUESTION

Turn your citizen's problem into a possibility. With all the new knowledge you have gained, write your own "what-if" question to share the possibility you see for the future of energy in City X.

HORSE POOP 9 FEET HIGH

THERE IS A popular saying that "necessity is the mother of invention." It means that new ideas, new innovations, and new inventions usually are created because there is a strong need for them. When we really, really need a solution to something, more people are likely to put their minds to it harder, so a solution will be created. As Irresistible Futures engineers, you are part of this too. Your inventions respond to the needs that the citizens of City X have.

▶ THE NEED TO THINK DIFFERENTLY

There is a common mistake when we try to create solutions: We focus on the problems. This is why, as an Irresistible Futures engineer, you are trained to think about a vision for the future instead. When we focus on problems, we try to *fix* them; we try to undo them; we think about the way things are and get upset and argue about why and how we can change it. But the real innovators think about the future and different ways of doing things that will eliminate problems altogether.

In this case study, we will learn about a very real problem that has been in our world for millions of years: poop.

CASE STUDY ///
THE GREAT HORSE MANURE CRISIS OF 1894

▸ ## HOW MUCH POOP IS TOO MUCH POOP?

In the late 1800s, the biggest cities in the world were growing fast. They had a lot of people living in them, and horses were the main source of energy used to move people and things around the cities.

And what do horses do? They poop.

We know that everybody poops, but horses poop a lot. In fact, one horse (just one!) makes up to 50 pounds (or more than 22 kilograms) of poop every day!

At the end of the 1800s, there were 50,000 horses in London and 100,000 horses in New York City. The poop that horses made in New York City in *one* day weighed more than *two* double-decker airplanes full of people.

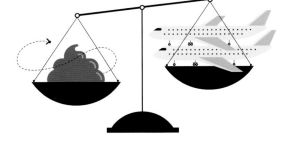

▸ ## THAT IS TOO MUCH POOP

The cities didn't know what to do. Poop was piling up, and they couldn't get rid of it. There is a story that the newspaper in London predicted every street in London would be buried under 9 feet (2.7 m) of manure in 50 years. (Manure is a boring adult word for poop.)

Nobody knows if the story about the newspaper is really true. But we do know there was a lot of poop, and people argued about what to do. Nobody could find a solution.

CASE STUDY (CONTINUED)

HORSE POOP 9 FEET HIGH

▸ UNTIL SOMEONE DID

You just learned in the previous activity about first principles thinking. The first principles of the poop problem were simple: What are the parts of the problem? Horses, poop, streets. What is the need? Getting people and things from one place to another.

The solution was found by looking at one of the first principles that was easier to solve than the fact that horses poop, and they came up with a vision for an irresistible future: What if we had transportation that didn't need horses?

Within 20 years, the poop problem didn't exist anymore. Cars, buses, trains, and airplanes carry us all around the world now.

Today, we hear about how the pollution from those vehicles is so bad that we are going to suffocate our planet. Some very smart engineers have already thought about the problem from first principles: The problem to focus on isn't getting *rid* of pollution. It's not making pollution in the first place. It's the energy we use to power those cars. So the irresistible future today is: What if we had cars that didn't burn fuel and pollute the atmosphere?

Electric cars are becoming more popular. What do you think the problem will be in another hundred years?

CASE STUDY /// G DIAPERS

You may think the poop problem is gone, but *human* poop piles up on our planet too! One company in Australia, called gDiapers, has an idea that just might help.

gDiapers is all about changing the way we catch baby poop. They invented the first home-compostable diaper that is made completely of materials and ingredients that can get absorbed right back into nature. So no dirty diapers piling up in the garbage!

But Kim and Jason, the parents of gDiapers, wanted to do more. They had a crazy idea. They asked, "What if we didn't think of diapers and poop as waste at all?"

What if our own human poop could be turned into something even more valuable?

▸ GCYCLE

The idea that gDiapers created is the first diaper in the world that is completely renewable. They deliver diapers to places that use them—like daycare centers or hospitals—and then pick them up again when they're used. Then they use advanced technology to change those diapers (and their poop!) into electricity!

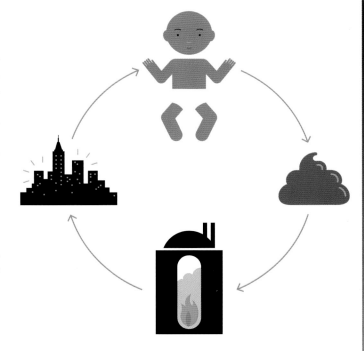

Kim and Jason are testing their idea around the world and are getting feedback to improve the process and make it even better.

In their irresistible future, gCycle diapers are free for everyone and **baby poop powers the world.**

TAKEAWAY

New solutions create new challenges too. But if you are creative, you can turn those challenges into opportunities.

——— IMAGINE ——— ACTIVITY ———

"THIS IS NOT A . . ."

YOU HAVE LEARNED already about building on the ideas of others. Sometimes the most exciting solutions are the ones that are sitting right in front of us and just haven't been used yet. In this activity you will learn a basic creativity exercise that helps imagine how everyday things could be used in different ways.

It will help to have a couple other people to play this game with, but you can do it on your own too!

PREPARATION

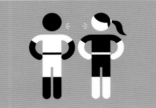

10 MINUTES

▶ WHAT YOU WILL NEED

▶ PREPARATION

The most important thing you need for this activity is an everyday object. For example, you could use a ruler, an empty paper tube, a box, a bag, whatever you find in your engineer kit or around your house. It's best to choose something simple and plain—not a picture or something with a lot of words or designs or details.

Gather a partner or two to play the game with and share your citizen's problem with them. Remember, we are working to imagine solutions to their energy challenge!

"THIS IS NOT A . . ."

The first step of the game is easy! You hold up the object you chose, look at it seriously, and declare to the world that *this* is not whatever it appears to be.

Then use your creative engineer brain to think of a way that it could be a solution to your citizen's problem. Inform your friends of what it *actually* is.

This is not a ruler!

PASS IT TO A FRIEND AND REPEAT

Pass your object back and forth between everyone playing and come up with as many ideas as you can. Everyone gets to imagine together, and you can build on each other's ideas to make new and crazy ones. Continue until you have at least ten ideas of what your object could be as a solution to your citizen's problem.

It is the blade of a wind power generator!

TAKE NOTES

Make a list in your notebook of all the solutions you come up with. If you would need to make changes to the design in order for it to work, that's okay! Write or draw notes next to each idea if you would need to adapt your object to be a good solution.

solutions

CHOOSE YOUR FAVORITE IDEA

In this challenge we are going to select two of our favorite ideas to continue with in the create stage. Which two did you think were best?

CREATE ACTIVITY

FOCUS GROUP

WHEN WE HAVE a few different options to choose from as we design solutions, a helpful way of deciding the best one to create is a focus group.

A focus group is a small number of people who are asked to test and give feedback on ideas. Companies use focus groups often to see how people like the ideas their engineers have imagined.

In this activity you will test both of your two favorite ideas from the Imagine stage.

PREPARATION

45 MINUTES

▶ WHAT YOU WILL NEED

▶ PREPARATION

Find a couple friends or family members who you can ask to be your focus group. Tell them about your citizen's challenge and everything you have learned so far. You will show them your solutions and ask them for feedback on both of them.

If you have two of the same object you used in the imagine stage, you can have your focus group look at both of them at the same time. If you only have one, then get feedback on the first idea, take it back to change it into the second, and ask for feedback a second time.

ADAPT YOUR OBJECT

Look back at your notes from the imagine stage. If you need to make any changes to your object in order to make it into a model of your solution, do that first! You can use your engineer kit to make your model.

Remember, you have two models to make! You can make them both at the same time if you have two of the object. Otherwise, you'll come back to this step later for the second model.

TEST YOUR FIRST SOLUTION

Give your first solution to your focus group. Ask them to imagine they are your citizen and to think about how this object would solve their problem. They can ask questions. They can touch it and feel it too.

Make notes using an improve and repeat page.

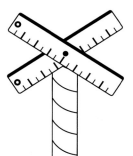

My solution is . . .

TEST YOUR SECOND SOLUTION

Repeat the process with your second solution. Ask your focus group the same things and listen carefully to their feedback.

YOUR BEST SOLUTION

Think about all the feedback and ideas you got and make a final solution that is even better than the first two. Remember, the best solutions often build on the ideas of others. This final solution can even combine your two ideas!

NAME YOUR SOLUTION

Make a drawing of your best solution in your notebook and be sure to give it a name!

MUSICALLY SPEAKING

IN THIS ACTIVITY you are going to share your solution through music. Don't worry, you won't need to find a whole band or get a professional singer. All you need is yourself and your favorite tune.

▶ **FLASH LEARNING**

You might wonder what music has to do with sharing the solution you designed. Think about commercials you watch on TV, the music that plays before a speaker steps to the microphone at an event, or even the little jingles for products that get stuck in your head. There is a reason that music is used to share ideas with others.

A lot of research has been done on the effect that music has on the human brain. In fact, some research shows that music activates more parts of your brain than anything else in the world—more than eating food, more than talking, more than playing a game, more than anything!

When you hear music, your brain actually works more! You are able to think better and be more creative, and because your whole brain works together, you can make connections faster and in new ways.

And the feelings that come from that excitement in your brain make music a great way to share our ideas in a way that makes people feel.

PREPARATION

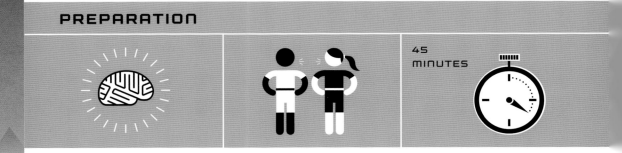

45 MINUTES

▶ WHAT YOU WILL NEED | ▶ BEFORE YOU START

Before you begin, listen to some music. Pick a song that you love or a song from when you were younger that makes you have good memories. Close your eyes and listen to the song, just once. This is to get your brain juices flowing and to get you feeling creative. Research tells us the effect of the music will last even after you finish listening!

PICK A TUNE

Think about the little songs that you hear when you watch a favorite TV show or the jingle that goes with a toy you love. Do you have a favorite?

Sing the tune to yourself or find it online and listen to it to have it fresh in your mind.

CHANGE THE WORDS

Now imagine the same tune is going to be used to share your solution with the world. Pretend it is the theme song for your own commercial or that it would be played every time someone uses your invention.

Remember to use the three-act story method to make sure you are telling the important parts of the story in your song.

PERFORM

Tell your family or friends about your invention and share your song with them. Hopefully it gets stuck in their head and they sing it the rest of the day. Then even more people will hear about your solution!

CONGRATULATIONS

You have helped create an irresistible future for **energy** in City X.

· THE ·
IRRESISTIBLE
FUTURES
AGENCY

7 DESIGN THE FUTURE OF SAFETY

ONE OF THE most important things in a city is keeping citizens and visitors safe. In our houses, our schools, and our cities, we have rules and people who make sure we follow them. We have signs to remind us of rules and people who can help us if someone else makes us feel unsafe. We also do things ourselves, like being careful when we walk outside and playing where we are supposed to. In City X, everyone comes from different places on Earth, and there are dangers that are very different from on Earth. How will you design a future of safety that will help everyone in City X live together peacefully and protected from the dangers of their new world?

The citizens of City X have asked you, the Irresistible Futures agent, to think about three main things when designing the future of safety:

ELEMENT 1: PERSONAL

Personal safety is about how you protect yourself. It can be a lot like protecting your health, too. When we feel safe, we can use our talents and our skills in the best ways to build the future we dream of. **How will you help the citizens of City X all feel safe and free from harm?**

ELEMENT 2: DIGITAL

We are all real people, but anyone who uses the internet or a computer is a digital person too—and we need to protect that person just the same. **How will you help the citizens of City X create a future where our digital world is just as safe as, or even safer than, our physical world?**

ELEMENT 3: PUBLIC

Public safety is about dangers that affect a lot of people. City X is on a new planet, so the safety of the city, but also the safety of the planet, is very important to think about. **How will you help the citizens of City X keep each other safe from danger both in the city and outside the planet?**

EXPLORE ———— ACTIVITY

SAFETY FIRST

YOU'VE PROBABLY HEARD an adult tell you before, "Safety first!"

Safety is a very important part of our lives, but we don't often think about all the things we have around us that are there to keep us safe.

In this activity you will spend a day carefully noticing all the things that keep us safe.

PREPARATION

1 DAY

▶ WHAT YOU WILL NEED

▶ PREPARATION

To complete this activity you don't need to do anything special. You just need to pay very close attention to everything around you for a whole day!

Ask an adult you trust to help pick a day that you can use to observe safety in your world. Then just go about your day as you normally would but with your design notebook close at hand. Very much like the first activity we did to notice transportation, this time you will notice all the things around you that keep you safe.

1 WHAT KEEPS YOU SAFE?

Before you start, make a list of all the things you can think of that keep you safe.

2 OBSERVE

Each time you notice one of these things throughout your day, make an X next to that thing. If you find more things that keep you safe, add them to the list and keep track of those too.

3 THINK ABOUT IT

At the end of the day, think about all the ways you were kept safe. Think about all the people who helped keep you safe, all the inventions that helped keep you safe, all the engineers who designed those solutions so that you and all your friends and family would stay safe!

Now you need to think like those engineers as you create a solution to keep citizens of City X safe too.

Here are some ideas to help you:

What about . . .

At home? In the car? On the street? While you eat? While you sleep? When you travel? While you learn? When you play?

my room
airbags
my shoes
night light

Let's create a solution to keep citizens of City X safe.

///

REFLECT

In your notebook, write down three things you learned about safety that you hadn't thought of before.

USER RESEARCH: TOWN HALL

SAFETY IS A public concern, and often our leaders and our laws can make a big difference in our safety. People usually agree about what being safe is but not always about what decisions help us get there.

In City X, the mayor tries to work very closely with the citizens to make new policies and laws, especially about safety. To learn more about what parts of life in City X are unsafe, the mayor held a town hall to hear opinions and respond to concerns. He invited everyone in City X to gather together and talk, and the head of public safety came to take notes about what everybody said. Here are some of the results of the town hall and a few specific challenges that citizens brought up.

RESULTS

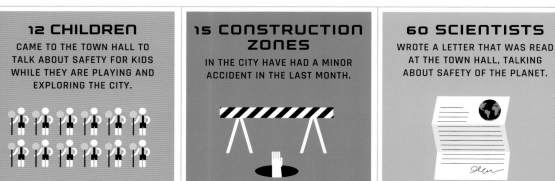

12 CHILDREN
CAME TO THE TOWN HALL TO TALK ABOUT SAFETY FOR KIDS WHILE THEY ARE PLAYING AND EXPLORING THE CITY.

15 CONSTRUCTION ZONES
IN THE CITY HAVE HAD A MINOR ACCIDENT IN THE LAST MONTH.

60 SCIENTISTS
WROTE A LETTER THAT WAS READ AT THE TOWN HALL, TALKING ABOUT SAFETY OF THE PLANET.

TOWN HALL

When a leader wants to know what people think, a **town hall** is a good way to do that. The term comes from a gathering place where the government of a town is located, but this kind of research can happen anywhere that is safe and convenient to meet. A leader will invite anyone who wants to attend to come and share their opinions on a challenge, and the leader's main job at a town hall is to listen and think about what is common between all of the perspectives and ideas that are shared.

A town hall is good for

1. Leaders who want to understand what the people they serve are thinking

2. Listening carefully

3. Helping create rules and policies together with other people

USER RESEARCH: CITIZEN PERSPECTIVES

JEREMIAH

"Will my grandkids be safe walking around City X?"

"I heard we live near an asteroid belt. What if an asteroid comes close to our planet?"

HELGA

NIKAU

"I want to have real-time connection but also want my privacy."

"Can we keep our society peaceful without police or military?"

LUCIA

LAJUANDA

"I go to work in virtual reality. How do I keep myself safe while I'm there and keep my virtual identity protected?"

WHICH CITIZEN OF CITY X WILL YOU DESIGN FOR?

As an Irresistible Futures agent, you will design a solution for one of these City X citizens. Who will it be?

1 Choose a citizen to design for.

2 How do you think your citizen is feeling? Choose from some of the words to the right or come up with your own.

AMAZED   DISAPPOINTED

BRAVE   SECURE

ISOLATED   ANXIOUS

AMUSED   SAFE

SYSTEMS THINKING

SYSTEMS THINKING IS a special kind of problem solving that engineers use. It is a way of thinking not just about a problem on its own but about the relationships between problems and with the world around them.

In fact you have been learning it throughout this whole book and didn't even know it!

You practiced finding the connections between problems.

You practiced breaking problems down into smaller parts.

You practiced thinking big and thinking carefully.

But one part of systems thinking you haven't learned yet is what we at Irresistible Futures call "circular solutions."

▶ **FLASH LEARNING**

Circular solutions are solutions that solve more than one problem, because they create a system. You learned in the energy challenge about a company called gDiapers. They built a circular solution!

PREPARATION

30 MINUTES

▶ WHAT YOU WILL NEED

▶ FIND A SECOND CHALLENGE

In order to build a circular solution, you need two challenges to solve at the same time. Your first step is to choose a second challenge.

For this activity you will use two citizens' challenges:

1 The citizen you chose for this safety challenge

2 The citizen you chose for the environment challenge (page 35)

Remind yourself of the problems that both citizens are facing—the citizen in this challenge and the citizen in your environment challenge. Forget about the solution you designed for the environment; we are starting fresh!

This is the most advanced kind of problem solving that Irresistible Futures engineers do. So roll up your sleeves and get ready to use everything you have learned to design a new circular solution.

1 COMBINE CHALLENGES

Think about your citizens' two problems. It might help to write them down next to each other.

Are there any parts of your safety challenge that also have to do with the environment? Remember all three components of environment: pollution, disasters, and the built environment.

Are there any parts of your environment challenge that also have to do with safety?

Remember all three components of safety: personal, digital, and public safety.

2 COMPARE CHALLENGES

What is similar about the two problems? What is different? Use the tools you have already learned to think about these problems carefully.

The why game, the four P's, or first principles may help you here!

3 INSIGHTS

Take careful notes as you combine and compare your challenges. Look over them when you are done and try to find the places where you can connect you problems with a circular solution.

WRITE YOUR "WHAT-IF..." QUESTION

Turn your citizen's problem into a possibility. With all the new knowledge you have gained, write your own "what-if" question to share the possibility you see for the future of environment and safety together in City X.

INNOVATION VS. INVENTION

WHEN YOU HEAR about engineers and designers, you will sometimes hear people talk about their solutions as *innovations* or *inventions*. Sometimes we think of the words the same way, to mean that we are coming up with something that nobody has ever thought of before. And that sounds really hard! With billions of smart people on Earth, a lot of things have been thought!

Understanding the difference can help you feel more confident as an engineer, whichever path you take. Inventing and innovating are both important parts of designing solutions.

▸ WHAT IS INVENTION?

Invention is really quite simple—coming up with something that nobody has ever made before. Usually invention uses a new process, a new material, or a new idea that never existed. The first time a human carved a stone into a wheel, that was an invention! The first time someone made a filament of the right kind of metal and put electricity into it, it lit up and the lightbulb was invented!

Invention can be very hard but also very exciting.

▸ WHAT IS INNOVATION?

Innovation is about building on the ideas of others. That's something you have practiced a lot as an Irresistible Futures agent. Innovators often use the first principles thinking that we learned about to put basic parts together in completely new ways. That can be parts of objects, parts of processes, or even parts of a school or a company. Innovation changes the way something is done.

Some of the best solutions are actually both! They use inventions together with innovations to make truly powerful solutions.

SAFETY

CASE STUDY

CASE STUDY /// SMARTPHONE

▶ INVENTION OR INNOVATION?

Think about the smartphones that so many people use. Are these phones an invention or an innovation?

We might think at first that they are an invention. After all, a lot of new parts were made to create them, and they didn't exist before. But all the things you can do on a phone—take photos, look at the internet, make a call, send a message—are things you could do before smartphones.

The phones are an innovation. The people who made the first smartphone took a whole lot of processes and put them together in one place to change the way that we use information in our lives. Now all of these tools are at our fingertips instead of in different places.

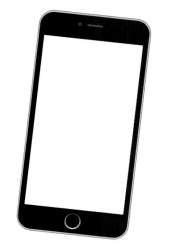

CASE STUDY /// THE INTERNET

▶ INVENTION OR INNOVATION?

But then think about something that the smartphone uses, like the internet. Before the internet, information was shared using paper and film. People had large sets of books in their homes that they used to look up words and information, and when you wanted to find information you didn't have at home, you would go to the library to find a book that had what you were looking for. When you wanted to send a letter to somebody, you would write it on paper and ask the post office to take it to them for you.

But with the internet, information became digital. It didn't live on paper anymore. It became something that could be shared and found immediately, and enabled communication that was instant and high quality. The internet was a completely new process, new material, and new idea that never existed before. It has probably been the most important invention in human history.

TAKEAWAY

As an Irresistible Futures engineer, you can both invent and innovate as you solve the challenges of City X.

127

IMAGINE — ACTIVITY

OUTSIDE THE BOX

THINKING OUTSIDE THE box is one of the best ways to come up with ideas. Let's try it as you come up with a solution for your City X citizen.

PREPARATION

45 MINUTES

▶ WHAT YOU WILL NEED

▶ THE DOT GAME

Can You Connect These Dots?

To start thinking outside the box, let's try a little brain puzzle. Draw nine dots in the center of a blank page in your design notebook, just like you see to the right.

Now try to connect all of the dots, without lifting your pencil from the paper, using only four straight lines. The lines have to be connected. Remember, you can't lift your pencil from the paper.

Go ahead! Try it!

When you find a way, or if you are still stuck after five tries, continue reading.

A Hint

Did you solve the puzzle yet? If you didn't, here's a hint:

The solution to the dot game is to think outside the box. Instead of focusing just on the nine dots themselves—focusing on the problem and the solutions everyone else would try—you need to look at the world around the problem, and use that extra space to come up with the answer.

This is the same thing you can do to imagine a new solution for your citizens' challenges. Remember that you are creating a circular solution to the problems of two citizens—from the safety challenge and the environment challenge.

1 CHOOSE YOUR WEAPON

By now you are an expert at imagining solutions. We have learned so many ways to think big. Choose your favorite way to come up with new ideas: making lists, using sticky notes, drawing pictures, taking a walk to let your mind expand—whatever worked the best for you!

2 THINK OUTSIDE THE BOX

Remember the example of a circular solution from the company making baby poop into power? That is outside-the-box thinking!

Imagine as many ways as you can to solve your citizens' problem with a circular solution—a solution that solves them both.

3 SYSTEM CHECK

Choose one or two ideas that you think are great. Then check that they are indeed circular solutions. Does your solution create a system and solve both problems?

IF YOU NEED HELP,
TRY THIS EXERCISE:

1. LOOK AROUND THE ROOM
    AND FIND THREE RANDOM
    THINGS.

2. PRACTICE THE "THIS IS
    NOT A . . ." ACTIVITY
    FROM THE ENERGY
    CHALLENGE.

3. IMAGINE HOW THESE
    OBJECTS MIGHT BECOME
    COMPLETELY UNIQUE
    SOLUTIONS.

CHOOSE YOUR FAVORITE IDEA

Choose your favorite circular solution and move on to create!

The Solution

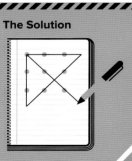

CREATE ACTIVITY

ENGINEER'S CHOICE

BY NOW YOU have learned so many ways to create and test a model of your solution. In this activity you will compare the different creation methods we learned and decide which one is the best for you to use as you design a circular solution for your citizens.

PREPARATION

30 MINUTES

▶ **WHAT YOU WILL NEED**

▶ **PREPARATION**

Remind yourself of your favorite solution, and assemble your engineer kit, just in case you need it.

1 PROS AND CONS

First think about all the different create activities you have completed. You have built models in so many ways. Make a list in your design notebook and make two other columns, one with a + on top and one with a −.

When an engineer has a lot of different possibilities to do something, they use critical thinking skills to decide which one is best for each problem they encounter. So for each of the create skills you learned, make notes about what you liked and disliked about each one. What you like, put on the + side; and what you didn't like, put on the − side. What made each one easy? What made each one hard?

2 CHOOSE THE BEST METHOD

As a skilled Irresistible Futures engineer, you can now choose the method of creation that you think will be best to make a model of your solution. Which one will do the best job of showing others what your idea is and how it works?

Choose your method and make your first model.

3 IMPROVE AND REPEAT

Ask for feedback—good things, questions, and things to change—from friends or an adult you trust. Improve your model, get feedback again, and make one final version.

NAME YOUR SOLUTION

Make a final version of your model based on all the feedback. What will you call your solution?

SHARE ACTIVITY

YOUR MOMENT OF FAME

THIS IS IT—YOUR last activity before you become an official Irresistible Futures agent. This is your moment of fame.

It's time to take everything you have learned and put it to the test, as you share your genius with the world one last time.

In this activity you will use all the tools you have learned so far, remembering how to tell a good story of your solution, how to put your user in the story, and the different ways of sharing your ideas in a way people will understand and remember.

Your final task is to make a video 2 minutes long that tells the story of your solution for the safety challenge in City X.

PREPARATION

3 HOURS

▸ **WHAT YOU WILL NEED**

▸ **NOTE**

If you don't have a camera or a phone that can record video, you can complete all the tasks on the next page; but instead of recording it at the end, just perform it for your friends or family!

1 THE THREE-ACT STORY

We'll start at the beginning, with the three-act story. Complete a three-act story page in your design notebook.

2 STORYBOARDING

Imagine how you would tell this story if it was a commercial or a short video. What would the different scenes look like? If you need a reminder, look at the share activity in the communication challenge.

In your design notebook, draw your storyboards for your video.

3 ROLE PLAYING

Write your script! What are the lines you are going to say in the video? Will you ask a friend or family member to be in the video with you? Can someone act as your City X citizen?

4 MUSICALLY SPEAKING

Write a short jingle that you can use to introduce your solution. You can include this at the beginning or the end of your video!

5 RECORD

Ask an adult you trust to help you make a video. Practice what you'll say and do in the video, how you will show your model of your solution, and how you will demonstrate it. Practice a couple of times so that when you record, it will be really good!

Watch the video after you are done. How did you do? This is what an engineer of an irresistible future looks like.

CONGRATULATIONS

You have completed the **safety** challenge, and you are officially an Irresistible Futures agent.

IRRESISTIBLE
FUTURES

OFFICIAL
AGENT

CONCLUSION

FROM: MAYOR OF CITY X

Dear Citizens of Earth,

We have received your transmissions and have begun building your solutions here in City X. Our citizens are thrilled with the creativity, beauty, and depth of your ideas and are excited for what our lives will soon be like here on our new home world.

Thank you for your dedication and your talent. You proved your skills while completing seven challenges and learned so much about how to explore, synthesize, imagine, create, and share solutions. You are welcome any time in City X, and we hope to see you here soon.

The challenges we face here in City X are quite similar to the challenges you face on Earth. I hope you will use your new skills to improve the place where you live too. You understand the challenges. You have the tools and knowledge you need and the technology to make it happen. All you need is *you*: your visions, your ideas, your creativity, and your solutions to the problems you face.

It is my honor to officially name you an Irresistible Futures agent.

The future of City X—and the future of humanity—is in *good* hands.

IRRESISTIBLE FUTURES

OFFICIAL AGENT

WHAT IS YOUR IRRESISTIBLE FUTURE?

NOW THAT YOU'RE an official Irresistible Futures Agent, it's time for you to create the future you want to see. This book, and all its lessons, is your toolkit. Use it well.

The Irresistible Futures Agency is real. It is a group of people all around the world—young and old, from this country and that—who are working to build a future that works. Welcome.

When you are ready to practice your new skills, remember these three steps:

1 **Pick a situation in your world that you would like to change.**

Find a problem you care about.

2 **Imagine the future you could create.**

Turn your problem into a possibility.

3 **Make that future happen.**

Use all your new skills to share your vision with others and bring it to life.

WE'LL SEE YOU IN THE FUTURE.

CONNECT WITH THE
IRRESISTIBLE FUTURES AGENCY

IRRESISTIBLEFUTURES.ORG

DOWNLOAD	SHARE	LEARN MORE
free educator resources for using this book in the classroom.	your visions for the future, and the inventions you created using this book.	about City X and becoming a designer of the future.

If you use social media, share your inventions and ideas from this book on your favorite platform using the hashtag **#irresistiblefutures**.

ACKNOWLEDGMENTS

CITY X WAS founded at the end of 2012, not as a physical city of course, but as a metaphorical place where young people around the world could design their own futures. What began as a series of haphazard experimental workshops with fourth-grade students in my small hometown in Wisconsin eventually grew into the City X Project, a problem-solving course that has since been used by hundreds of thousands of kids in a dozen languages in over 75 countries.

Through the City X Project, we sought to create a story and a world where everyone could see themselves—where City X could be any city, anywhere; where the characters were representative of all the people in our lives, with varied backgrounds, cultures, identities, and abilities. We worked with partners around the world to craft a learning experience that was tested in many "realities," from the tundra of Alaska to the metropolis of Hong Kong to a mountaintop children's home in Lebanon. Our course even left Earth to go to the International Space Station, minting the world's youngest space engineer, as you learned about in this book.

As we return to City X for an entirely new adventure, it is this foundation we build upon, and I want to acknowledge the city's other founders, Libby Falck and Matthew Straub. Libby, Matthew, and I clocked countless late nights and hundreds of thousands of air miles as we built this world together. Libby led our project, and it was her ideas, drive, and connections that brought the City X Project into its very existence. Matthew told the story of our world in myriad ways, from pixels to newspapers. You'll see several of his photos throughout this book. Libby and Matthew, thank you for the experience of crafting this world together, for the lessons we now get to share, and for trusting me to build on our story and bring City X to life in a new way.

The original City X Project course is available to educators worldwide as a free Open Education Resource at cityxproject.com.

BRETT SCHILKE IS a storyteller, curriculum designer, and education theorist who builds experiences that redefine learning for the future. He does super adultish things in non-adultish ways, like teaching at a university, designing museums, and helping governments and schools all around the world change the way people learn. He does it all while wearing multi-colored shoes, giving way too many high fives, and throwing single-song dance parties for his co-workers.

Brett lives in Palo Alto, California.

brettschilke.com

INDEX

A

Accessibility in transportation, 19
Accidental innovation, 58–59
Agriculture, 67

B

Balanced diets, 67
Biomimicry, 42
Blueprinting, 62–63
Built environment, 35

C

Case studies
    about, 11
    communication, 58–59
    energy, 108–111
    environment, 42–43
    food, 74–77
    health, 92–93
    safety, 126–127
    transportation, 26–27
Challenges, components of, 73
Circular solutions, 124–125
Commercials, 82–83
Communication
    basics, 51
    case studies, 58–59
    designing solution, 58–68
    elements of, 51
    exploration stage, 52–53
    imagining stage, 60–61
    sharing stage, 64–65
    synthesis stage, 56–57
    testing stage, 62–63
    understanding challenge, 51–57
    user research, 54–55
Components of challenges, 73
Constraint, psychology of, 94

D

Data, described, 104
Data analysis, described, 104
Delivery of energy, 101
Design notebooks, about, 17
Design process stages
    1. explore, 13
    2. synthesize, 13
    3. imagine, 13
    4. create and test, 13
    5. share, 13
    overview of, 11
    tools needed, 16
Digital safety, 119
Disasters and environment, 35

E

Efficiency in transportation, 19
Emotional health, 85
Empathy web, 68–69
Energy
    basics, 101
    case studies, 108–111
    designing solution, 108–117

elements of, 101
exploration stage, 102–103
imagining stage, 112–113
sharing stage, 116–117
synthesis stage, 106–107
testing stage, 114–115
understanding challenge, 101–107
user research, 104–105
Engineers, as designers of solutions, 10
Environment
    basics, 35
    case studies, 42–43
    designing solution, 42–49
    elements of, 35
    exploration stage, 36–37
    imagining stage, 44–45
    sharing stage, 48–49
    synthesis stage, 40–41
    testing stage, 46–47
    understanding challenge, 35–41
    user research, 38–39

F
First principles thinking, 106–107, 110
Flash learning, 98, 116
Food
    basics, 67
    case studies, 74–77
    designing solution, 74–83
    elements of, 67
    exploration stage, 68–69
    imaging stage, 78–79
    sharing stage, 82–83

    synthesis stage, 72–73
    testing stage, 80–81
    understanding challenge, 67–73
    user research, 70–71
Four P's, 72–73

H
Health
    basics, 85
    case studies, 92–93
    designing solution, 94–99
    elements of, 85
    exploration stage, 86–87
    imagining stage, 94–95
    sharing stage, 98–99
    synthesis stage, 90–91
    testing stage, 96–97
    understanding challenge, 85–91
    user research, 88–89

I
Innovation
    accidental, 58–59
    described, 126, 127
Invention, described, 126, 127
Irresistible, definition of, 10
Irresistible Futures Agency
    challenges, 14
    described, 10, 136
    design process, 13
Iteration, described, 30

L

Language of communication, 51
Letter writing, 54

M

Medical needles, 43
Medium of communication, 51
Mistakes, 59
Music and flash learning, 116

N

Notebooks, about, 17
Nutrition, 67

P

Parts of challenges, 73
Patterns in challenges, 73
Penicillin, 58
People in challenges, 73
Personal problems, described, 15
Personal safety, 119
Perspectives, importance of understanding
    different, 26
Play-Doh, 59
Point of service research, 88
Pollution and environment, 35
Poop problems, 108–111
Population and food, 67
Presence of communication, 51
Prevention and health, 85
Problem maps, 56, 68
Problem solving
    beginning, 28
    thinking methods, 11
    using imagination, 28–29
    "What if" questions, 24–25
Problems
    in challenges, 73
    types of, 15
Psychology of constraint, 94
Public safety, 119

R

Research types
    data analysis, 104
    letter writing, 54
    point of service, 88
    surveys, 22
    town halls, 122
    voting, 38
    word on the street, 70

S

Safety
    basics, 119
    case studies, 126–127
    designing solution, 126–133
    elements of, 119
    exploration stage, 120–121
    imagining stage, 128–129
    sharing stage, 132–133
    synthesis stage, 124–125
    testing stage, 130–131
    understanding challenge, 119–125
    user research, 122–123
SBAR, 90–91
Social problems, described, 15
Speed in transportation, 19
Storage of energy, 101
Storyboards, 64–65
Surveys, about, 22
Sustainability and energy, 101
Systems thinking, 124

T

Thinking outside the box, 128, 129
"The Three-Act Story" method of sharing,
    32–33
Town hall research, 122
Transportation
    basics, 19
    biomimicry, 42
    case study, 26–27
    designing solution, 26–33
    elements of, 19
    exploration stage, 20–23

imaging stage, 28–29
sharing stage, 32–33
synthesis stage, 24–25
testing stage, 30–31
understanding challenge, 19–25
user research, 22–23
Treatment and health, 85
TV commercials, 82–83

U

User research
communication, 54–55
described, 11
energy, 104–105
environment, 38–39
food, 70–71
health, 88–89
importance of understanding different
   perspectives, 26
safety, 122–123
transportation, 22–23
See also Case studies

U

Velcro, invention of, 43
Voting, as type of research, 38

W

"What-if" questions, 24–25
"What's in My Head" Game, 52–53
Word on the street research, 70

ALSO AVAILABLE

3D Printing and Maker Lab for Kids
978-1-63159-799-2

Astronomy Lab for Kids
978-1-63159-134-1

Creative Coding in Python
978-1-63159-581-3

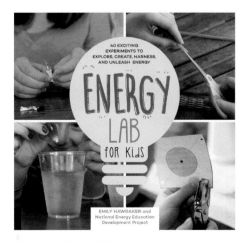

Energy Lab for Kids
978-1-63159-250-8